Applied Tarot Reversed

A Practical Guide to Interpreting *Reversed* Tarot Cards

by Emily Paper

Applied Divination
Redmond

Published by Applied Divination

ISBN 978-1-7356170-7-7

Front cover image by Emily Paper
Illustrations by Emily Paper
Photographs from Unsplash.com
Book design by Emily Paper

First printing edition 2021

Applied Divination
www.applieddivination.com
info@applieddivination.com

Contents

Introduction

What are Reversed Tarot Cards?

Reversed cards are cards that land upside-down. That's it, that's all! Maybe you pulled one on purpose. Maybe you shuffled and turned half the deck around without meaning to. Maybe you meant to. Maybe a card fell out of the deck and landed askew. Either way, you have an upside-down card and now you need to do something with it.

For *applied* or practical reasons, reversals are often even more useful than upright cards.

For example, when I lost my car keys a few years ago and pulled the reversed King of Pentacles as my first tarot card, I immediately recognized it as "smashing the patriarchy." That's what a reversed King means to me.

Upright, the King has a variety of meanings that I would've had to figure out - such as happiness, success, generosity, a giving man, a helpful older gentleman, or the masculine facets of my own self. How do I find car keys with that information? Reversed, it's just smashing the patriarchy - something I do every day!

As mentioned in my previous book, *Applied Tarot*, together with some other cards I was able to locate my missing keys in my daughter's jacket. My female offspring smashes the patriarchy even better than I do, so it all worked out.

Where did *you* lose *your* keys? Let the Reversed Tarot cards tell you!

A Quick Reference for Interpreting Reversals

I use reversed cards in all of my daily readings. However, their interpretation can sometimes be much more involved and highly dependent on upon the querent and the question.

This book is intended to be an extremely simplistic view of each reversed card, but the meanings as they apply to you might be very involved.

Here are a few simple ways to incorporate reversals:

1. Interpret the cards as the exact opposite of its upright meaning. For example, if you are looking for something to eat and draw The Hanged One upright, it would tell you to suck it up and eat leftovers. A reversed Hanged One might suggest you go nuts with food delivery!

2. Interpret the cards as being more specific to your situation or location. For example, if you are looking for a place to travel and draw The Star upright, it suggests you visit Stonehenge. A reversed interpretation might be to go find (or build your own) stone statues instead.

3. Interpret the card with a more negative meaning (or positive if the card upright is traditionally negative.) For example, if you were wondering what part of your house to clean and you drew the Six of Cups, upright it suggests you tidy the kids' playroom. A reversed interpretation might be to scrub their dirtiest toys, instead. The point is still taking care of kid toys, but it is slightly less fun.

4. Interpret it as a look back at the upright card that precedes it in the deck. For example, if you draw the reversed Six of Wands (upright: an event of victory), check the meaning of the Five of wands (Struggle and competition) and realize that perhaps you are not a victor, but that your fans are suggestion you move on.

One more trick for reversals
Imagine the image in the card is real life, and you've completely turned it upside down. What would happen to the character? Examples:
- The Magician would drop all his tools (No skills, unused talents)
- The Seven of Swords thief would drop his loot (Confession, getting caught)
- The Page of Cups would spill his cup (broken heart, vulnerability)

How to use this book

Think of this book as a reference, not a novel. You do not need to read it front to back, nor should you. This book is for answering simple questions with tarot cards, and assumes you have a tarot deck on hand.[14]

Steps:
1. Ask your question.
2. Shuffle the deck and pull a card.
3. If your card is reversed, skip to the page in this book intended for the card pulled, and hopefully you will get some functional insight.
4. If your card is upright, read my first book, *Applied Tarot*, available on Amazon[15]

If you *do not* get any functional insight, you can attempt a wordier answer by using the combinations calculator on Page 100.

Finally, understand that if the individual card interpretations do not help, or the combinations calculator spews randomness, your question might not have a simple answer and you might need to figure things out on your own. Good luck with that!

A quick note on movie recommendations: A good movie falls into several themes, so take my suggestions lightly. These are all movies that are fairly well known, ones I have personally seen, and which fit the card category listed. Do not be offended by my movie choices - For example, I prefer MCU over DC and your tastes might be different - read the entire meaning and choose your own book or movie that fits the theme.

If you have movie or book recommendations, contact me through www.applieddivination.com

---

[14] If you do not own a Tarot deck, I highly recommend The Gilded Tarot or the Rider-Waite Tarot (available at bookstores near you), or my deck, the Applied Tarot (available through my website)

[15] US readers can get a discounted paperback copy of Applied Tarot through my website, with free shipping! Visit http://emilypaper.com/store/p6/appliedtarotDISCOUNT

About the Deck Images in this Book

The US copyright owner for the Rider-Waite wanted money for the classic RW iconography, but I'm too stubborn and cheap for that. Instead, I created my own cards with similar imagery. Photo credits in the back.

This deck is available for purchase on emilypaper.com.

The Major Arcana Reversed

ꞁooℲ ǝɥ┴

O

The Fool reversed is recklessness, naivety, or
other tom*fool*ery. Upside down, this baby lacks
stability and direction, and will fall.

0
The Fool Reversed

The Fool upright dances through the hilltops without direction, his faithful pup by his side. Upright, the Fool card asks us to take a risk and make a leap. Trust yourself.

Although this card is generally about starting something new, when reversed it could represent poor judgment or a foolish decision. With Major Arcana there are always a number of interpretations for what could be happening in a reversed position. Figure out which one is correct for you:

1. You may be bounding into something without first stopping to weigh the pros and cons.
2. You may be talking yourself out of something before you begin. What are you afraid of?
3. You may be so in love with starting new things, you fail to commit to growing in one specific area.
4. You are NOT taking a leap when you should be. What is holding you back?

Questions answered by the Fool reversed:

>**Who**? A naïve or reckless person
>**What**? A thoughtless action
>**Where**? Somewhere dangerous
>**When**? Immediately; January and February
>**Why**? "Carefulness costs you nothing. Carelessness may cost you your life." ~Unknown
>**Yes or No**? Maybe – stop and consider it first

The reversed Fool
>**Before any card:** Don't jump into (card)
>**After any card:** Reckless Behavior

The Fool Reversed as:

...an action
- Stop and think about things
- Walk the dog
- Dive deep into skills you already have

...a place in your house?
- The floor
- Downstairs

...a place in your city?
- Somewhere you visit frequently
- A pet store
- A children's museum

...a place in the world?
- The sea
- A famous valley, such as the Valley of the Ten Peaks (Canada) or Yosemite (USA)
- The Grand Canyon

...something to eat?
- Applesauce
- Oats or granola

...something to clean?
- Clutter on the floor
- Give the baby or pet a bath

...where to find the missing item?
- On the floor somewhere

...a color? White, Yellow

...a movie theme? Avoiding danger, rushing into things
- About Time
- Safety Not Guaranteed

...a new career?
- Join an established company with good benefits
- Working with animals, babies, or pets

Possible Major Arcana combinations with The Fool reversed:

> **Upright Magician:** brilliant but careless
> **Reversed High Priestess:** not listening to intuition results in being taken advantage of
> **Upright Empress:** an insecure or worried parent
> **Reversed Emperor:** a reckless tyrant
> **Upright Hierophant:** archaic harmful traditions
> **Reversed Lovers:** partnership ends too quickly
> **Upright Chariot:** not being cautious on a trip
> **Reversed Strength:** Insecurity leads to one being taken advantage of
> **Upright Hermit:** a wise person doubts themself
> **Reversed Wheel:** a risk leads to bad luck
> **Upright Justice:** consider cause and effect
> **Reversed Hanged One:** faking martyrdom
> **Upright Death:** impulsive ends
> **Reversed Temperance:** extremely careless
> **Upright Devil:** a drug addict, inconsideration
> **Reversed Tower:** trying everything to avoid disaster
> **Upright Star:** blind faith
> **Reversed Moon:** thoughtlessness and confusion
> **Upright Sun:** carefree abandon, childhood joy
> **Reversed Judgement:** a lack of self-awareness
> **Upright World:** Fear of success

The Major Arcana represent significant life events. The Fool reversed could be:

- A failed start to a new venture
- A career change requiring deep thought
- Downsizing a house or career
- A divorce
- A fall or tumble

Uh-oh dummy - that's what happens when you don't pay attention.

The Magician

I

The Magician reversed has the skills of the upright card, but uses them for manipulation or greed, or may be confused about their use.

I
The Magician Reversed

The upright Magician is an all-knowing, all powerful person. They have every tool they need readily at their fingertips. Tools might be something we *know*, something we *have*, or something we *are*.

In reverse, the Magician may not know how to use these powers, or might use them for manipulation, greed, or deviousness. Imagine a stage Magician dropping or losing all of their tools – not much of a magician now, are they?

Reversed, this card is generally about business, but there are a few things that could also be happening:

1. You may be manipulating someone.
2. You may be having trouble connecting goals with the actions needed to achieve them.
3. You could be envious of someone else who seems easily able to achieve their dreams.
4. You or someone is acting unethically.

Questions answered by the Magician reversed:

Who? A brilliant manipulator out of place for her or his age or position; an actual magician
What? A deviant behavior
Where? Somewhere mysterious, like Area 51
When? Soon; May and June; August and September
Why? "Until you realize how easy it is for your mind to be manipulated, you remain the puppet of someone else's game." ~ Evita Ochel
Yes or No? No, or change your tactics

The reversed Magician
Before any card: Obtain more skills in (card)
After any card: Evil, deviance

The reversed Magician as:

...an action?
- Take big steps toward long term goals
- Take a chance on something new and bold
- Learn a magic trick

...a place in your house?
- The office
- The closets
- A crafts area
- The workshop

...a place in your city?
- A magic shop
- The library
- A craft store
- A school

...a place in the world?
- Egypt
- Italy
- India
- A haunted house

...something to eat?
- Potato chips
- Garlic
- Donuts
- Deli meat

...something to clean?
- The most cluttered drawer or closet
- Your home office

...where to find the missing item?
- Where you last had a wicked thought
- The dining table

...a color? Dark red, blue, purple

...a movie theme? Magic or manipulation
- The Prestige
- Point Break
- Now You See Me

...a new career?
- Magician
- Construction
- IT helpdesk
- Amateur bowler
- Villain

Possible Major Arcana combinations with The Magician reversed:

Reversed Fool: An inconsiderate swindler
Upright High Priestess: Out of touch with one's inner voice
Reversed Empress: A nosy manipulator
Upright Emperor: An insecure father
Reversed Hierophant: A rebellion
Upright Lovers: Someone in a partnership is engaging in trickery or deviance
Reversed Chariot: No planning or direction
Upright Strength: Confident yet unfocused
Reversed Hermit: a lonesome villain
Upright Wheel: A period of misused skills
Reversed Justice: Dishonest, unfair
Upright Hanged One: A confusing sacrifice
Reversed Death: An extreme fear of change
Upright Temperance: One must be patient with the unknown
Reversed Devil: Breaking free of tricks
Upright Tower: A villain causes disaster
Reversed Star: Hopelessness, insecurity
Upright Moon: everything is an illusion
Reversed Sun: Unhappiness, needs therapy
Upright Judgement: karma catches up
Reversed World: A lack of skills leads to incompletion of projects

The Major Arcana represent significant life events. The reversed Magician could indicate:

- A manipulative person coming into your life, or you become them
- A life event requiring more skills
- An illusion

Oh no, where'd your magic stuff go, buddy?

14

The High Priestess

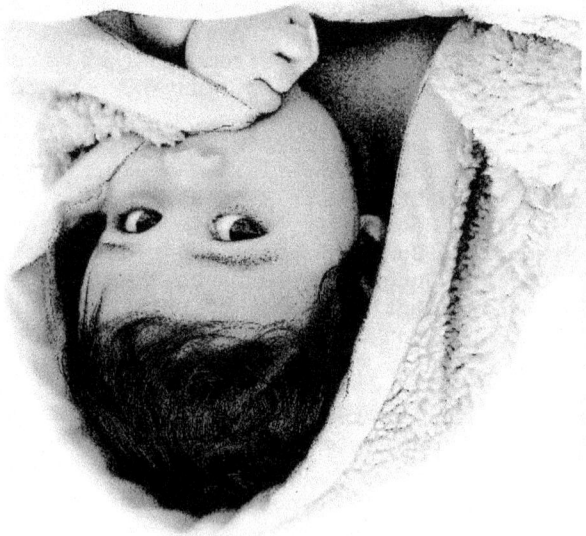

||

The High Priestess reversed isn't listening to their intuition. Think of an upside-down baby – they are helpless and emotional.

II
The High Priestess Reversed

The High Priestess upright is intuitive and looks inside herself for the truth, rather than seeking answers from outside. The Priestess is often a teacher, guide, or wise source of psychic information.

In reverse, you still need to look inward, perhaps even more so than before. Some piece of information might be missing, or you could be feeling detached from others. Make sure you have all the details and are kept in the loop.

There are a few other things that could be happening here when the Priestess is reversed. Figure out which one is correct for you:

1. You're not trusting yourself.
2. You're too emotional to deal with your issues right now.
3. Your intuition is or was wrong, and you can't trust it now.
4. Someone is keeping you out of the loop.
5. You're losing faith in something.

Questions answered by the High Priestess Reversed:

Who? Your subconscious; an emotional person
What? An emotional outburst; tension
Where? In your own head
When? In the gloaming or twilight; During a full moon; June and July
Why? "A quieted mind can hear intuition over fear." ~ Anonymous
Yes or No? No

The reversed High Priestess
Before any card: You have doubts about (card)
After any card: doubt, fear

The High Priestess reversed as:

...an action?
- Calm down
- Exercise
- Write down your thoughts

...a place in your house?
- The bookshelf
- The bathroom

...a place in your city?
- A fitness class
- A school
- A therapist's office

...a place in the world?
- Peru
- The Middle East
- The Philippines

...something to eat?
- Whatever you are craving
- Bacon
- Coffee

...what should I clean?
- The gutters, eaves, or sills
- The outside of the windows

...where to find the missing item?
- Outside
- Near a window

...a color? Turquoise, coral, orange

...a movie theme? Trusting oneself, high emotions
- The Dark Knight Rises
- The Greatest Showman
- Hidden Figures

...a new career?
- Personal coach or therapist
- Artist
- Clergy
- A position in Academia, ex: professor

Possible Major Arcana combinations with The High Priestess reversed:

Upright Fool: Jumping in without thinking
Reversed Magician: feeling of inadequacy
Upright Empress: emotional overflow
Reversed Emperor: a cold, thoughtless man
Upright Hierophant: conformity causes a loss of self
Reversed Lovers: a one-sided relationship
Upright Chariot: an emotional journey
Reversed Strength: self-doubt, insecurity
Upright Hermit: listen to one's inner voice
Reversed Wheel: loss of situational control
Upright Justice: difficulty accepting the truth
Reversed Hanged One: stalling
Upright Death: difficulty accepting an end
Reversed Temperance: extreme imbalances
Upright Devil: an emotional affair
Reversed Tower: must find inner strength to avoid disaster
Upright Star: a search for hope and trust
Reversed Moon: extreme fear or anxiety
Upright Sun: joyful disregard for intuition
Reversed Judgement: complete failure to listen to the self
Upright World: failure to notice signs from the universe

The Major Arcana represent significant life events. The reversed Priestess could indicate:

- A gut feeling you're not listening to
- Dirty laundry (real or metaphorical)
- An uncontainable emotional outburst

Something isn't right here. Put your thinking cap on straight and figure it out.

The Empress

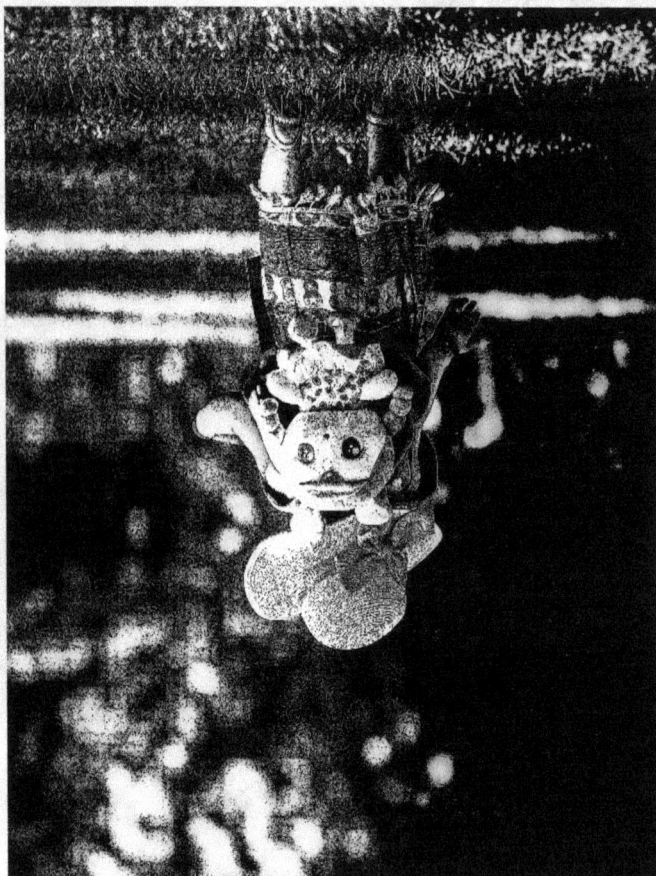

III

The Empress reversed is a smothering parent, a
burned out and frustrated worker, or someone
buried in clutter and blocked creativity.

III
The Empress Reversed

The Empress upright is the Earth Mother. She has the biggest and most compassionate heart, and gives of herself freely, sometimes to her own detriment.

The Empress reversed may have bitten off even more than she can chew. Alternatively, she's put far too much of herself out there in the world and now there are too many pieces to pick up (literally, in the form of clutter, or figuratively, the form of too many things going on at once.)

Here are a few things the reversed Empress could imply:

1. Either a very smothering "helicopter" parent, or one who doesn't care at all (two sides of the same coin, neither is good)
2. You may be buried under clutter and need a Spring cleaning
3. Trouble with one's parent or parent figure
4. A need to trust one's gut

Questions answered by the Empress reversed:

> **Who?** An overbearing person or parent
> **What?** Overindulgence or malnourishment
> **Where?** A group home; a retirement home; the baby's room
> **When?** When the leaves change; a death; The beginning of Spring; The beginning of Autumn
> **Why?** "a lot of parents will do anything for their kids, except let them be themselves." ~Banksy
> **Yes or No?** First change your attitude or behavior

The reversed Empress
> **Before any card:** Smothering or stifling (card)
> **After any card:** Emptiness, infertility

The Empress reversed as:

...an action?
- Have a nap or eat a healthy meal
- Explore your feelings about babies or starting a new project

...a place in your house?
- The office
- The freezer
- An ice machine
- The weeds

...a place in your city?
- A prison or court
- A funeral home
- The mall

...a place in the world?
- Haiti
- The Congo
- Siberia
- Iceland

...something to eat?
- Fast food
- Beer
- Potato chips
- Granola bars

...something to clean?
- Declutter all surfaces
- The nursery

...where to find the missing item?
- The youngest household member has them

...a color? Red, chartreuse, blue

...a movie theme? Smothering parents
- Bad Moms
- LadyBird
- Monster in Law

...a new career?
- Accountant
- A work from home job
- Government job
- Doggie daycare or vet work

Possible Major Arcana combinations with The Empress reversed:

Reversed Fool: An enabler, infertility
Upright Magician: Using talents for manipulation
Reversed Priestess: Repressed emotions
Upright Emperor: A smothering father
Reversed Hierophant: Cult-like religion
Upright Lovers: Codependence
Reversed Chariot: Zero emotional control
Upright Strength: Compassion fatigue
Reversed Hermit: Loneliness
Upright Wheel: A change causes emptiness
Reversed Justice: An unjust system
Upright Hanged One: Martyrdom, narcissism
Reversed Death: Anxiety about change
Upright Temperance: Need to balance emotion
Reversed Devil: Difficulty with control
Upright Tower: Disaster; storm; distress
Reversed Star: Discouragement
Upright Moon: Listen to the subconscious
Reversed Sun: Negative person, pessimist
Upright Judgement: Childfree; infertile
Reversed World: No closure; emptiness

The Major Arcana represent significant life events. The Empress reversed could indicate:

- An infertile or childfree couple
- A violent weather system
- A helicopter mom
- Climate change
- A death

Poor mama, you got yourself all flip-turned upside down.

The Emperor

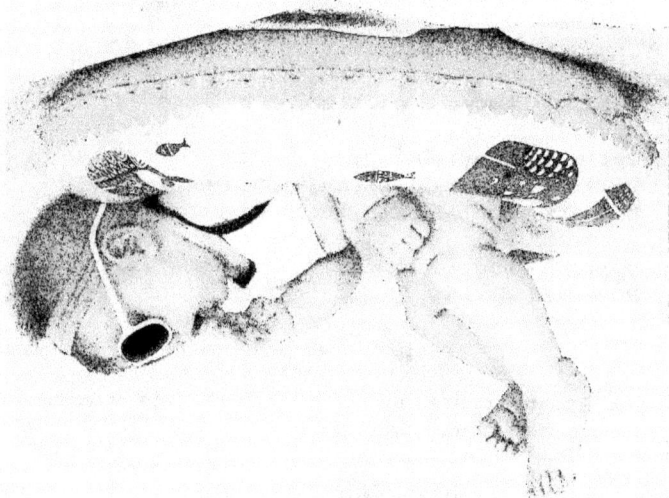

IV

The Emperor reversed is an emperor to the extreme - he is a manipulative control freak, or authoritarian rather than authoritative.

IV
The Emperor Reversed

The upright Emperor is a father figure or strong masculine influence. Typically, he is older, stable, wise, and protective.

But reversed, he may become these things to an uncontrollable extreme, such as an abusive male from a patriarchal upbringing, or a quick-tempered illogical man. When the Emperor card appears reversed, it is important to know how to protect yourself from this strong negative influence (even if - especially if - it's coming from you!)

A few other things could be happening here:

1. A person lacking the knowledge or skills to be a good leader; a cruel boss
2. Abuse; the patriarchy in general
3. Work that is overwhelming or too difficult
4. Someone who needs more feminine influence

Questions answered by the Emperor reversed:

Who? An authoritarian leader; a difficult male
What? A task that is too difficult or stressful
Where? A government office
When? Unexpectedly abrupt; The start of Spring; Aries
Why? "Uneasy lies the head that wears a crown" ~ Shakespeare
Yes or No? No

The reversed Emperor
Before any card: Unskilled, authoritarian (card)
After any card: Authoritarianism, tyranny

The Emperor reversed as:

...an action?
- Make a plan
- Call your dad
- Practice saying "no."

...a place in your house?
- An authoritative chair
- The phone

...a place in your city?
- The courts
- An arena
- The Police station

...a place in the world?
- Washington DC
- The U.A.E
- The Middle East
- North Korea

...something to eat?
- Steak
- Meat from an animal you hunted yourself
- Booze

...something to clean?
- The microwave
- The garage

...where to find the missing item?
- Under a pile of bills
- In the kitchen
- A masculine individual has them

...a color? Pink, yellow, pastel

...a movie theme? Authoritarianism
- The Godfather
- Judge Dredd
- The Hunger Games

...a new career?
- Military
- Police
- International Management
- Government work

Possible Major Arcana combinations with The Emperor reversed:

Upright Fool: An insecure and tyrannical boss
Reversed Magician: A manipulative trickster
Upright Priestess: Possibly negative self-talk
Reversed Empress: An abusive relationship
Upright Hierophant: Structured authority, the Patriarchy
Reversed Lovers: disharmony in a partnership
Upright Chariot: Rigidity, too much structure
Reversed Strength: Weakness; overreaction
Upright Hermit: Retreat; a step back
Reversed Wheel: Repeating the same mistakes
Upright Justice: Justice prevails, good or bad
Reversed Hanged One: A male feigns martyrdom
Upright Death: The end to abuse
Reversed Temperance: tyrannical government
Upright Devil: An addict
Reversed Tower: Breaking of the glass ceiling
Upright Star: Renewed hope after disappointment
Reversed Moon: A big job for a confused leader
Upright Sun: Defeating The Man brings joy
Reversed Judgement: A reckoning for one's behavior
Upright World: An anti-hero

The Major Arcana represent significant life events. The Emperor reversed could indicate:

- A difficult boss or loss of job
- A devastating defeat
- Being overpowered

Dude is still upright, he's just a lot meaner. But he's not carrying the big stick anymore so you have a shot here.

The Hierophant

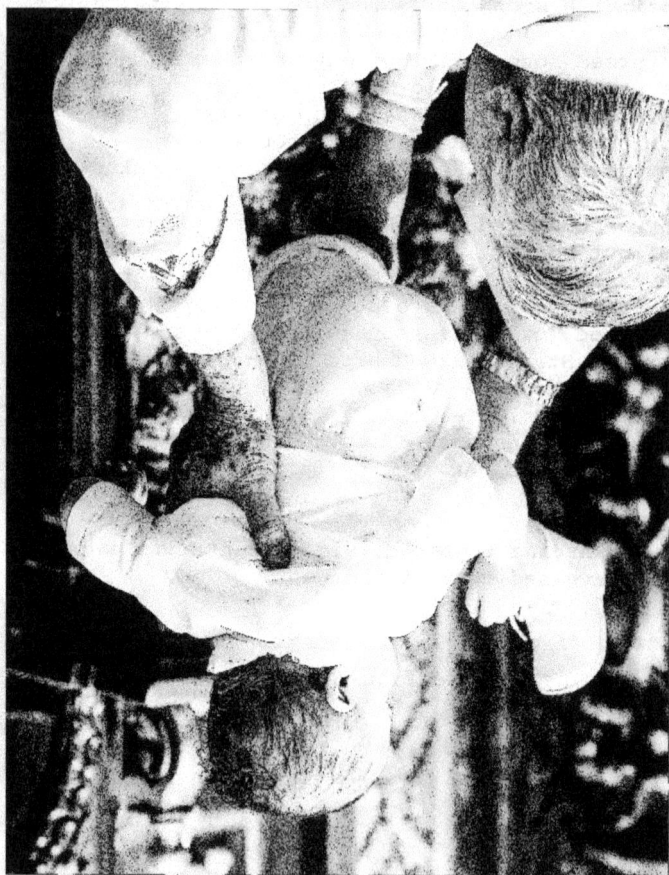

∨

The Hierophant is about tradition, business,
and conformity. Reversed, it is rebellion –
the baby fights to break free of tradition!

V
The Hierophant Reversed

The Hierophant upright follows rules from an established tradition, possibly ones created years ago by a strict and authoritative patriarchy. When the card is pulled upright it could be talking about a traditional event, such as a wedding or baptism, or it could be about following the rules and not stepping out of line.

When the Hierophant is reversed, it typically represents rebellion, questioning the rules, or even doing your best to smash the patriarchy. There might be some other things at play as well. Figure out which one is correct for you:

1. Progressive rebellion and non-conformity
2. Something that goes against your morals
3. Relationship problems
4. Bad advice, or good advice you should have listened to but didn't

Questions answered by the reversed Hierophant:

> **Who?** An unconventional teacher, or surprising guidance
> **What?** A rebellion
> **Where?** A farm or wage workplace
> **When?** April and May; During the rebellion
> **Why?** "If you think adventure is dangerous, try routine; it is lethal." ~ Paulo Coelho
> **Yes or no?** Maybe, it depends on circumstance

The Hierophant reversed
> **Before any card:** Taking an unconventional approach to (card)
> **After any card:** Rebellion, poor relationships

The Hierophant reversed as:

...an action?
- Examine your usual way of doing things
- Disobey
- Listen to your conscience

...a place in your house?
- The garage
- Arts or music space

...a place in your city?
- An art museum
- A park
- A new denomination of church

...a place in the world?
- Northern India
- Hong Kong
- Tibet
- France

...something to eat?
- Asian Fusion
- Cronuts
- Unsliced bread

...something to clean?
- The playroom
- The newest items purchased
- A shelf of occult wares, such as crystals or idols

...where to find the missing item?
- In a pile of the latest clutter
- With the fun and games

...a color? Canary Yellow, Tangerine, dark blue

...a movie theme? Rebellion; Abuse of power
- Robin Hood
- The Matrix
- Silicon Valley (TV, HBO)

...a new career?
- Rebel leader
- Reporter/journalist
- Writer or artist
- Teacher

Possible Major Arcana combinations with The Hierophant reversed:

> **Reversed Fool:** Reckless and unsafe rebellion
> **Upright Magician:** Creative new use of talents
> **Reversed Priestess:** Reexamine limiting beliefs
> **Upright Empress:** Nature finds a way
> **Reversed Emperor:** Revolt against tyranny
> **Upright Lovers:** A new approach to relationship
> **Reversed Chariot:** Directionless rebellion
> **Upright Strength:** Finding strength to fight back
> **Reversed Hermit:** Societal outcast
> **Upright Wheel:** New approaches to old problems
> **Reversed Justice:** Lack of accountability, lies
> **Upright Hanged One:** Sacrificing oneself for tradition
> **Reversed Death:** Fear of what must be done
> **Upright Temperance:** finding your own meaning
> **Reversed Devil:** Atheism, rejection of church
> **Upright Tower:** Overthrow of traditional values
> **Reversed Star:** Losing faith
> **Upright Moon:** Subconscious rebellion
> **Reversed Sun:** Fights and quarrels, depression
> **Upright Judgement:** Reawakening to one's purpose
> **Reversed World:** A time-out from everyday life

The Major Arcana represent significant life events. The Hierophant reversed could indicate:

- Disobedience and rebellion
- Challenging beliefs or traditions
- Marital problems or divorce
- Destructive advice

Trust me. I'm not a regular priest, I'm a cool priest!

The Lovers

VI

The Lovers reversed is disharmony, conflict, and disconnection. This could be with a partner or between one's own head and heart.

VI
The Lovers Reversed

The upright Lovers sometimes represents a symbiotic relationship, a marriage, or otherwise wonderful union. More often than not, however, it represents the perfect synchronicity between one's head and heart. When faced with a major life decision, the upright lovers tells us that our brain and our heart are in sync with whatever we decide.

Reversed, it is a split, a bad choice, or something else that is mainly negative. Figure out which meaning applies to your situation:

1. Divorce, disharmony
2. Inner conflict. A disconnect between what your head knows and what your heart wants
3. Conflict, imbalance, arguments
4. A need to consider ones values and ethics

Questions answered by The reversed Lovers:

Who? Your ex; someone you disagree with
What? A conflict
Where? Divorce court; the bar; a dating app
When? May to June; Sagittarius astrological sign; A slow burn
Why? "We exhaust ourselves more from the tension and the consequences of internal disharmony than from hard, unremitting work." ~Stephen Covey
Yes or No? No

The Lovers reversed
Before any card: A misalignment of (card)
After any card: disharmony; imbalance

The Lovers reversed as:

...an action?
- Realign your lifestyle with your values
- Apologize to your partner

...a place in your house?
- The pantry
- The family room

...a place in your city?
- The dog park
- The office
- A nail salon

...a place in the world?
- Reno, Nevada
- The Maldives
- Belarus

...something to eat?
- Dried fruit
- A TV dinner
- Fajitas for one

...something to clean?
- The dining table
- The kitchen
- The area with the most junk

...where to find the missing item?
- The place you were last alone

...a color? Cerulean, turquoise, black

...a movie theme? Divorce, values misalignment
- Marriage Story
- Just Go With It

...a new career?
- Divorce lawyer
- Matchmaker
- Sole proprietor, freelancer
- Auditor

Possible Major Arcana combinations with The Lovers reversed:

Upright Fool: Naivete in relationships
Reversed Magician: Lack of skills, or a mismatch of talents
Upright Priestess: Valid mistrust of a partner
Reversed Empress: nosy person; a falling out
Upright Emperor: Structure favors one partner
Reversed Hierophant: A falling out with structures or the church
Upright Chariot: One partner has all control
Reversed Strength: a relationship is insecure
Upright Hermit: Single by choice; online dates
Reversed Wheel: Bad luck in love
Upright Justice: Truth breaks up a partnership
Reversed Hanged One: One partner sacrifices themselves far more than the other partner
Upright Death: An end to a bad relationship
Reversed Temperance: extreme lack of balance
Upright Devil: A narcissist
Reversed Tower: Disharmony destroys a company
Upright Star: A need for communication
Reversed Moon: The head and the heart are miles apart
Upright Sun: A happy single life
Reversed Judgement: Lack of self-awareness
Upright World: Opposites attract; odd union

The Major Arcana represent significant life events. The Lovers reversed could indicate:

- A divorce
- A failed business partnership
- Misalignment between the head and the heart

This was a bad idea. I Don't think it's going to work out.

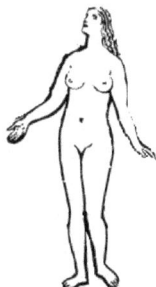

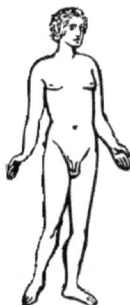

Probs true.

The Chariot

VII

The Chariot reversed is about immobility and a lack of direction. Imagine the baby's chariot flipped over - it cannot go anywhere.

VII
The Chariot Reversed

The Chariot upright is about choosing a direction and going for it, having ambition and determination, overcoming obstacles, or being victorious after hard work.

Reversed, imagine your personal chariot is overturned – there is no direction, the energies (and car parts) are scattered across the highway, and you are immobile and unable to move. That's a reversed chariot.

There may be other interpretations that fit, as well. Figure out which one is correct for you:

1. Immobility
2. A difficult decision is completely up to you
3. The wrong choice was made recently
4. A couple needs to take the next step in their relationship

Questions answered by the reversed Chariot:

> **Who?** Someone who needs car repairs; A mechanic; an unathletic person
> **What?** Self-doubt
> **Where?** A casino; a dead end; an overgrown forest
> **When?** A full moon; daytime; June and July
> **Why?** "If you do not change direction, you may end up where you are heading." ~Lao Tzu
> **Yes or No?** No, unless you choose a different way

The Chariot reversed
> **Before any card:** A choice must be made about (card)
> **After any card:** indecision; lack of direction

The Chariot reversed as:

...an action?
- Stay home
- Take the car in for repairs
- Change direction

...a place in your house?
- The sofa
- Storage and clutter area

...a place in your city?
- A car repair shop
- A prison

...a place in the world?
- Point Nemo
- The South Pacific
- Los Angeles
- Rio de Janeiro

...something to eat?
- Gas station sushi
- Candy
- Pineapple on pizza
- Fast food

...something to clean?
- The shoe storage

...where to find the missing item?
- In your shoes

...a color? Green; white

...a movie theme? Indecision; staying home
- Mr. Nobody
- Hamlet
- Home Alone

...a new career?
- Transport driver, long haul trucker, or dispatcher
- Freelancer
- Special education teacher
- Career advisor

Possible Major Arcana combinations with The Chariot reversed:

> **Reversed Fool:** Jumping in without a plan
> **Upright Magician:** Skills not being used well
> **Reversed Priestess:** Lack of self-control
> **Upright Empress:** Indecision about a baby
> **Reversed Emperor:** Rigid, immobile structure
> **Upright Hierophant:** Morals play a role
> **Reversed Lovers:** A failing relationship
> **Upright Strength:** Weighing a difficult choice
> **Reversed Hermit:** Someone has lost their way
> **Upright Wheel:** Constant change in life path
> **Reversed Justice:** Unfair choices
> **Upright Hanged One:** Unwilling or unable to make a choice
> **Reversed Death:** Fear of making the wrong decision
> **Upright Temperance:** Taking the easy road
> **Reversed Devil:** Questioning everything
> **Upright Tower:** Indecision leads to upheaval
> **Reversed Star:** Refusal to listen to oneself
> **Upright Moon:** All paths ahead are difficult
> **Reversed Sun:** Indecision leads to depression
> **Upright Judgement:** A legacy of indecision
> **Reversed World:** Lack of choice means no closure

The Major Arcana represent significant life events. The Chariot reversed could indicate:

- A cancelled trip
- A broken-down vehicle
- Indecision

Uh, dude, where's my lions?

38

Strength

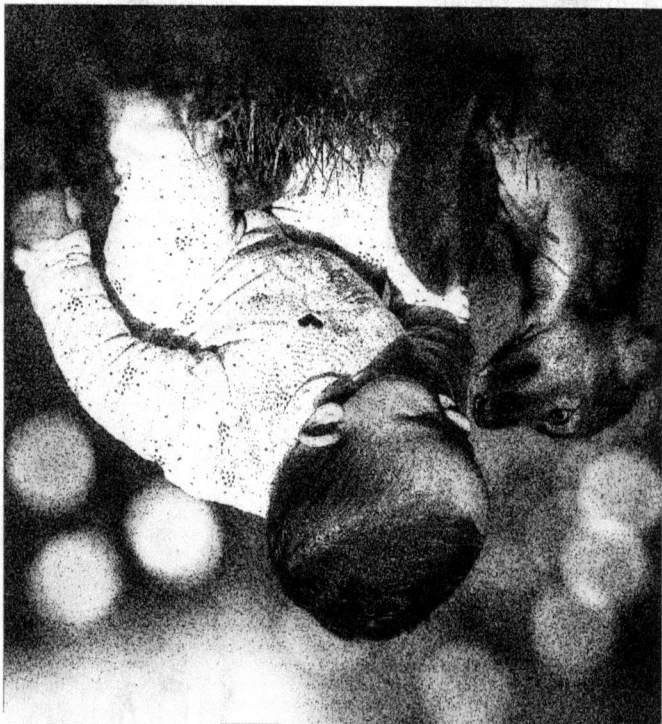

VIII

Strength reversed is doubt, weakness, and
vulnerability. Imagine dangling helplessly in
front of a feral animal.

VIII
Strength Reversed

The upright Strength card is about your inner will, confidence, and the animalistic nature that is inside all of us. When this card is upright, we can control our emotions, and deal with our problems with kindness, confidence, and compassion.

Reversed, there is a weakness which could be physical or emotional. We are vulnerable and lack self-recognition or control over our demons. There are many things at play when Strength is reversed, here are a few things that might be correct for you:

1. Weakness and vulnerability
2. Raw, uncontrolled animalistic instincts
3. Aggression
4. Reconsidering one's life direction

Questions answered by reversed Strength:

Who? A bum; a weakling; Someone who needs more confidence
What? Self-doubt; weakness; vanity
Where? The candy store
When? July-August; During sad times
Why? "All cruelty springs from weakness." ~Seneca
Yes or No? No. You are not prepared

Strength reversed
Before any card: A lack of confidence about (card)
After any card: Weakness, guilt

Strength reversed as:

...an action?
- Eat junk food
- Be lazy
- Seek help for your addictions

...a place in your house?
- Unused gym equipment
- The kitchen
- Storage

...a place in your city?
- A fast-food restaurant
- The pet store
- A gym

...a place in the world?
- Turkey
- Venezuela
- Greece
- Singapore

Something to eat?
- Highly caffeinated drinks
- Sweets
- Foods found low to the ground, such as carrots or potatoes

...something to clean?
- Exercise equipment
- The fridge
- The pet's food or litter box

...where to find the missing item?
- In the fridge
- The pet has them

A color? Pistachio, lemon yellow

A movie theme? Weakness, vanity
- Ocean's Twelve
- Carol
- The Social Network

A new career?
- Movie extra
- Dog walker
- Safety and Compliance inspector
- Epidemiologist

Possible Major Arcana combinations with Strength reversed:

Upright Fool: Self-doubt in a new project
Reversed Magician: Cowardice, being tricked
Upright Priestess: One's inner voice is weak
Reversed Empress: Insecure mother or parent
Upright Emperor: Being controlled by authority
Reversed Hierophant: Layoff; rejection
Upright Lovers: Weak in the knees for a lover
Reversed Chariot: Doubt in which path to take
Upright Hermit: Taking time out to regain strength
Reversed Wheel: Vulnerable to bad choices
Upright Justice: The truth is overwhelming
Reversed Hanged One: A wasted sacrifice
Upright Death: Fear of change
Reversed Temperance: Extreme weakness
Upright Devil: Someone else causes weakness
Reversed Tower: A whistleblower
Upright Star: Vulnerable to one's instincts
Reversed Moon: Too scared to travel
Upright Sun: A laughing fit; one is easy prey
Reversed Judgement: This is not your destiny
Upright World: Too scared to complete a mission

The Major Arcana represent significant life events. Strength reversed could indicate:

- A situation requiring willpower
- Laziness
- A sick pet
- Fear

Ouch, my butt!
Damn cat.

The Hermit

XI

The Hermit upright withdraws for study and
introspection. Reversed, there is isolation,
stress, and sadness.

IX
The Hermit Reversed

The Hermit upright is a time for inner reflection away from the hustle and bustle of the outside world. This card is all about solitude, soul-searching, spending time alone (maybe up in the mountains!) or finding enlightenment.

Reversed, often the quiet solitude has become overwhelming and turned into loneliness and sadness. Perhaps you are being anti-social or holier-than-thou to the point where no one wants to spend time with you.

There could be some other interpretations as well. Figure out which one is correct for you:

1. Loneliness
2. Exile
3. Looking for answers outside oneself
4. A need for self confidence

Questions answered by the Hermit reversed:

Who? A celebrity; an employee; a needy person
What? Eviction; deportation; rejection
Where? Out in public; Exposed
When? August-September; When connections are made; later
Why? "We allow our ignorance to prevail upon us and make us think we can survive alone, alone in patches, alone in groups, alone in races, even alone in genders."
~Maya Angelou
Yes or No? Probably not

The reversed Hermit
Before any card: Seek advice about (card)
After any card: Loneliness, ignorance

The Hermit reversed as:

...an action?
- Plan a date, even if it's with yourself
- Call a friend
- Study something new

...a place in your house?
- The bookshelf or library
- Outside the house, such as the front lawn or driveway

...a place in your city?
- A public park
- An isolation chamber

...a place in the world?
- Valleys
- French Polynesia
- A music festival

...something to eat?
- Pizza
- Juice
- Middle Eastern Cuisine

...something to clean?
- The deck; the front porch; the lawn

...where to find the missing item?
- The front porch
- The last place you were lonely

...a color? Neon green, bright yellow, Orange

...a movie theme? Exile, loneliness
- Cast Away
- The Lion King
- The Truman Show

...a new career?
- Librarian
- Embalmer
- Parking enforcement

Possible Major Arcana combinations with The Hermit reversed:

Reversed Fool: An irritable or moody person
Upright Magician: A desire to break free
Reversed Priestess: A loss of inner wisdom
Upright Empress: A single parent
Reversed Emperor: Cold and uncaring authority
Upright Hierophant: Conformity is isolating
Reversed Lovers: The loss of connections
Upright Chariot: Travel plans go awry
Reversed Strength: Depression and loneliness
Upright Wheel: The cycle of loss and gain
Reversed Justice: Criminal behavior
Upright Hanged One: Choosing to work alone
Reversed Death: Stagnation; loss
Upright Temperance: Finding meaning
Reversed Devil: Hard battle against addiction
Upright Tower: Sudden disaster affects a single person
Reversed Star: A lack of hope for any resolution
Upright Moon: Seek advice before a decision
Reversed Sun: Negative thinking; pessimism
Upright Judgement: Taking a break from one's life purpose
Reversed World: An incomplete goal

The Major Arcana represent significant life events. The Hermit reversed could indicate:

• Loneliness
• Isolation
• Depression

It kinda feels like everyone is having fun without me.

Wheel of Fortune

X

The Wheel is the cycle of life - sometimes it
is great, and sometimes everything collapses.
Reversed, it's usually a rough spot.

X
Wheel of Fortune Reversed

The Wheel of Fortune, upright or reversed, is exactly as it sounds - In most decks it will possess an image of a giant wheel, often with all the symbols of the tarot (and perhaps astrology) inscribed upon it. It represents the endless cycle of bad luck and good luck that is ever present in our lives.

There is a reason it is one of the middle cards in the Major Arcana - it is a turning point, and life will continue to turn no matter what happens. One moment you are up, and the next moment you are down.

Reversed, it's generally a negative part of this ever-turning cycle of life. Figure out what might be happening for you:

1. Bad luck
2. Events are out of your control
3. Failure
4. Change is necessary

Questions answered by the reversed Wheel of Fortune:

Who? Someone going through a rough time
What? A wheel; cancelled travel plans
Where? The casino; a big wheel
When? November-December; downtime
Why? "If you have bad luck at the dawn, you had bad luck. If you keep having bad luck all day, you are the bad luck." ~Amit Kalantri
Yes or No? No

The Wheel of Fortune reversed
Before any card: Bad luck in (card)
After any card: ruined travel; bad luck

The Wheel of Fortune reversed as:

...an action?
- Pause, slow down, or cancel travel
- Don't take that risk

...a place in your house?
- The broken vehicle
- The floor
- The bed

...a place in your city?
- The casino
- The auto repair shop
- A junk yard

...a place in the world?
- Vegas, Atlantic City, Monaco
- Citta-slow cities (cities in the slow-paced movement), like Grumes Italy or Sonoma, California

...something to eat?
- Mushrooms
- Cheese
- Vintage wine
- Tofu

...something to clean?
- The car

...where to find the missing item?
- On a circular thing

...a color? Red, blue, green, yellow

...a movie theme? Bad luck, slowness, life cycles
- Doctor Strange
- Arrival
- Rent

...a new career?
- Do not jump into a new career right now
- Casino work

Possible Major Arcana combinations with The Wheel of Fortune reversed:

Upright Fool: Failed attempts to start anew
Reversed Magician: Bad luck, poor skills
Upright Priestess: A bad gut feeling
Reversed Empress: A period of infertility
Upright Emperor: Negative business association
Reversed Hierophant: rejection of tradition has
   negative consequences
Upright Lovers: A relationship needs a break
Reversed Chariot: It is dangerous to travel
Upright Strength: The only way out is through
Reversed Hermit: isolation and self-doubt
Upright Justice: No control over the outcome
Reversed Hanged One: Stalling; dysfunction
Upright Death: One has no control over the end
Reversed Temperance: Bad financial period
Upright Devil: Time will reveal one's weakness
Reversed Tower: Bad luck for a small business
Upright Star: Cut your losses and move on
Reversed Moon: The trip will not go as planned
Upright Sun: Progress toward happiness is slow
Reversed Judgement: From bad to worse
Upright World: Taking small steps toward completion

The Major Arcana represent significant life events. The Wheel reversed could indicate:

- A time of bad luck
- A difficult period of time (ex: a bad year)
- An unfortunate event
- Ruined travel plans
-

I don't like these
odds. Can I have
another spin?

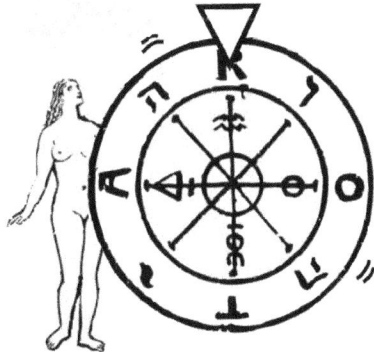

Justice

XI

Justice is law and order and getting what is
deserved. Reversed, order is not restored.
There is unfairness and no accountability.

XI
Justice Reversed

Justice in either direction is the purveyor of truth and honesty. In almost every deck she bears the scales, weighing right and wrong, and declaring that if you've been good, good things will happen to you. If you have been bad, well - you know.

When Justice is reversed, it's the bad side of your legal troubles. It may be time to pay the price for the wrongs you have committed, or it could be that the wrongs that have been committed against you will be rectified.

A few things could be happening with Justice Reversed. Figure out which might be true for you:

1. Injustice
2. Avoidance of the truth
3. Unfairness
4. Life is out of balance

Questions answered by reversed Justice:

Who? A criminal; An unjust judge or jury
What? Injustice
Where? A courtroom; an unbuilt structure
When? A time of denial; September-October
Why? "He who permits himself to tell a lie once, finds it much easier to do it the second time." ~ Thomas Jefferson
Yes or No? No, not until justice is restored

Justice reversed
Before any card: Unfairness in (card)
After any card: Injustice, dishonesty

Justice reversed as:

…an action?
- Apologize for any wrongdoings
- Pay your bills

…a place in your house?
- The bathroom or kitchen scale (literal)
- A teetering pile of clutter or books

…a place in your city?
- The prison
- A beginning yoga class

…a place in the world?
- The highest court
- Centra Africa
- Venezuela

…something to eat?
- Carbs
- Bacon

…something to clean?
- Pay off creditors
- Right anything that is wrong

…where to find the missing item?
- Near something that is out of place

…a color? Rust

…a movie theme? Injustice, lies, dishonesty
- The Invention of Lying
- The Usual Suspects
- Liar Liar

A new career?
- Lobbyist
- Fox news reporter
- Lawyer
- Politician
- Advertising executive

Possible Major Arcana combinations with Justice reversed:

> **Reversed Fool:** A reckless youth; an old liar
> **Upright Magician:** A highly skilled thief
> **Reversed Priestess:** Negative self-talk
> **Upright Empress:** An inheritance of dishonest means
> **Reversed Emperor:** Tyrannical abuse
> **Upright Hierophant:** Tradition is unjust
> **Reversed Lovers:** Infidelity; partnership ends
> **Upright Chariot:** A boat ride; imbalanced trip
> **Reversed Strength:** Vulnerable to loss or thievery
> **Upright Hermit:** Seeking the truth is difficult
> **Reversed Wheel:** Balance will not be restored
> **Upright Hanged One:** The scapegoat
> **Reversed Death:** Refusing to be held accountable
> **Upright Temperance:** Stoicism while facing lies
> **Reversed Devil:** Freedom from imprisonment
> **Upright Tower:** An intervention restores justice
> **Reversed Star:** Faithlessness in karmic justice
> **Upright Moon:** A guilty conscience
> **Reversed Sun:** Life isn't fair
> **Upright Judgement:** Remembering injustices and attempts at karmic restoration
> **Reversed World:** No justice is obtained

The Major Arcana represent significant life events. Justice reversed could indicate:

- Breaking the law
- Karma catching up to a person
- Lies
- Too overweight or underweight

Uh oh, lady justice isn't happy. You're in trouble now.

The Hanged One

XII

The Hanged One upright is patience and
sacrifice, but reversed it is the worst parts
of that - martyrdom and an inability to change

XII
The Hanged One Reversed

When upright, the Hanged One is typically about a person who often sacrifices themself temporarily, usually for the greater good. However, if can also be about feeling trapped or uncertain about which way to go.

Reversed, one might sacrifice him or herself with a feeling of martyrdom and with an expectation of reward, or there could be some other things at play.

The Hanged One is a multifaceted card that is hard to interpret on its own. One of these interpretations might apply to you:

1. Apathy or disinterest in issues
2. Stagnation or an inability to change
3. Martyrdom, sacrifice for the wrong reasons
4. Negative behaviors

Questions answered by The Hanged One reversed:

>**Who?** A detached or disinterested person
>**What?** Egotistical behaviors
>**Where?** In one's own head
>**When?** February-March; A period of stagnation
>**Why?** "You don't have to attend every argument you're invited to." ~unknown
>**Yes or No?** Probably not

The reversed Hanged One
>**Before any card:** Hypocrisy surrounding (card)
>**After any card:** Deception, fraud, martyrdom

The Hanged One reversed as:

...an action?
- Stop thinking about material things
- Focus on someone else

...a place in your house?
- The front hall closet
- The freezer

...a place in your city?
- A prison
- The cemetery
- Goodwill or the Salvation Army

...a place in the world?
- Iran
- A 3rd world country
- Rome
- London, UK

...something to eat?
- Gruel
- Pork
- Food that others in the household do not want to eat

...something to clean?
- Old storage cabinets, lockers, or rooms
- Dust the door frames and things above you that are not often visible

...where to find the missing item?
- Where you last stood still
- Somebody took them

...a color? Canary yellow

...a movie theme? Martyrdom, deception
- Mad Max: Fury Road
- Interstellar
- Macbeth
- Westworld (TV)

...a new career?
- Church job
- Superhero
- A job you're overqualified for
- Quit and do nothing

Possible Major Arcana combinations with The Hanged One reversed:

Upright Fool: Fear of starting something new
Reversed Magician: Deceptive, dishonest person
Upright Priestess: Resistance, delays
Reversed Empress: "helicopter mom"
Upright Emperor: A sacrifice for fatherhood
Reversed Hierophant: Sabotage, insurrection
Upright Lovers: Unsupportive partner
Reversed Chariot: Purposeful misdirection
Upright Strength: Bravery in the face of delay
Reversed Hermit: Fear of losing oneself
Upright Wheel: Delaying change a little longer
Reversed Justice: Jail time
Upright Death: A needless sacrifice
Reversed Temperance: Illness
Upright Devil: Suicide
Reversed Tower: Phobia
Upright Star: Hope for better outcomes
Reversed Moon: Uncertain outcomes
Upright Sun: A revelation or release brings joy
Reversed Judgement: Ignoring one's calling
Upright World: A regretful sacrifice for the greater good

The Major Arcana represent significant life events. Hanged One reversed could indicate:

- A fraud
- A victim complex, martyrdom
- A hypocrite or humiliated person
- Something important drops and breaks

Oh yay, I'm upright again.
...Waitaminute, why am I still all
tied up in this mess?

Death

XIII

Death upright is disruption, transformation,
or the end of a situation. Reversed, the baby
is unable to cope. There is loss, even death.

XIII
Death Reversed

The upright Death card is about chaos and transformation. It is a genuinely positive card, depending on how you view endings and beginnings, and tells us that if we can fight through changes, we'll come out as bigger, better versions of ourselves.

The reversed position is Death's terrible meaning. It is a devastating change - one that is hard to recover from - such as a major loss, upheaval, or even a death itself.

There are a few other things that could be happening here. Figure out which one is correct for you:

1. A resistance to inevitable change
2. A personal transformation
3. Disappointment
4. Stagnation

Questions answered by the reversed Death:

Who? A dying person; someone resistant to change
What? A death
Where? A room that has stayed the same; a funeral; Russia
When? October-November; after a delay; after a death
Why? "He who rejects change is the architect of decay. The only human institution which rejects progress is the cemetery." ~Harold Wilson
Yes or No? No

Death reversed
Before any card: Inability to accept (card)
After any card: Loss; defeat; delays

Death reversed as:

...an action?
- Get over it
- Slow down
- Confront fears
- Burn a bridge

...a place in your house?
- Piles of clutter
- The basement
- The medicine cabinet

...a place in your city?
- The morgue
- A bridge
- An old employer
- A funeral home

...a place in the world?
- Ponte de Barcas, Porto Portugal
- UAE
- Florida

...something to eat?
- Leftovers
- What you ate yesterday
- An apple
- Something new

...something to clean?
- Remodel or rearrange furniture
- Check the basement for rats

...where to find the missing item?
- Under furniture
- Where there is death or decay

...a color? White, grey, greige, tan

...a movie theme? Resistance to change; death
- A James Bond film
- Soul
- Toy Story
- Ghost

...a new career?
- Army
- CSI
- Zoologist
- Auditor, accountant
- Factory work

Possible Major Arcana combinations with Death reversed:

Reversed Fool: A reckless decision
Upright Magician: Being ghosted; ghosting
Reversed Priestess: Sadness; grief; regret
Upright Empress: Lateness; baby is overdue
Reversed Emperor: Trouble at work; firing
Upright Hierophant: Unwilling to follow rules
Reversed Lovers: Separation, divorce
Upright Chariot: Difficult but vital journey
Reversed Strength: Illness; death
Upright Hermit: Unwillingness to accept truth
Reversed Wheel: There is nothing you can do
Upright Justice: Justice resolves after delay
Reversed Hanged One: Victim mentality
Upright Temperance: Impatience; fear of delay
Reversed Devil: Relapse; overdose
Upright Tower: Delays after a sudden disaster
Reversed Star: Discouragement; insecurity
Upright Moon: Unconscious fears
Reversed Sun: Disappointments; loss
Upright Judgement: A difficult problem is resolved
Reversed World: A person unable to finish what they've started

The Major Arcana represent significant life events. Death reversed could indicate:

- Disappointment
- Death
- Burning bridges
- Running away from troubles

Trust me it's better
this way – you won't
feel a thing.

Temperance

XIV

Temperance reversed is imbalance and excess.
The water spills everywhere when the
Temperance card is flipped upside down.

XIV
Temperance Reversed

Temperance upright, commonly depicted as an angel pouring equal parts of water between two cups, reminds us to stay calm during turmoil. It foretells of a peaceful and patient time, where we are able to get some perspective and find our inner calm.

In reverse, however, something is out of balance in our situations and lives. Perhaps the querent is rushing into a decision without thinking it through, clashing with an antagonist instead of trying to find a compromise, or being hasty in a decision that requires thoughtful contemplation.

There are a few other things that could possibly be happening here:

1. Imbalance causing mistakes or misconduct
2. A need to back down and re-align the self
3. Greed, excess
4. A change is required

Questions answered by the reversed Temperance:

Who? An aggressive or reactionary person
What? Emotional turmoil
Where? Where a spill or flood occurs
When? November to December; During a flood or rainstorm; Without notice
Why? "When we are no longer able to change a situation, we are challenged to change ourselves" ~ Viktor Frankl
Yes or No? Not yet, work is needed

Temperance reversed
Before any card: Control your emotions about (card)
After any card: imbalance, mental illness

Temperance reversed as:

...an action?
- Make gradual changes
- Compromise
- Ask for help

...a place in your house?
- Bed
- The stovetop
- The faucet

...a place in your city?
- The beach
- The bank
- A dance studio

...a place in the world?
- Victoria or Niagara Falls
- Mount St. Helens or Pompeii
- Persia

...something to eat?
- Grapes
- Beans, Minute rice, other fast items
- Fast food

...something to clean?
- Don't clean today; have a nap instead

...where to find the missing item?
- In the couch cushions

...a color? Red, grape

...a movie theme? Impatience; sensitivity; flood
- Monsoon Wedding
- Booksmart
- Poseidon

...a new career?
- Writer or Author
- Trades like welding or plumbing
- Freelancer
- Veterinary assistant

Possible Major Arcana combinations with Temperance reversed:

Upright Fool: Not watching where you're going
Reversed Magician: Sabotage; deceit
Upright Priestess: Subconscious warning
Reversed Empress: Bad weather; growth delayed
Upright Emperor: A male figure is struggling
Reversed Hierophant: A rebellious teenager
Upright Lovers: A very emotional connection
Reversed Chariot: Bad weather disrupts travel
Upright Strength: Trying to control emotions
Reversed Hermit: Loneliness; mental illness
Upright Wheel: Extreme changes; bipolarity
Reversed Justice: A crime of passion
Upright Hanged One: A needless sacrifice
Reversed Death: Extreme changes; bipolarity
Upright Devil: Selfishness; greed
Reversed Tower: Chaos is temporary
Upright Star: Some difficulty finding hope
Reversed Moon: An emotional journey; therapy
Upright Sun: Mania or Manic disorder
Reversed Judgement: Refusal to listen to wisdom from those around you
Upright World: The mind is over-saturated

The Major Arcana represent significant life events. Temperance reversed could indicate:

- A difficult emotional period
- An inability to reach consensus
- A terrible flood, Tsunami, or storm

Oh no, I spilled everything and my feet are all muddy and this is just a catastrophe!

The Devil

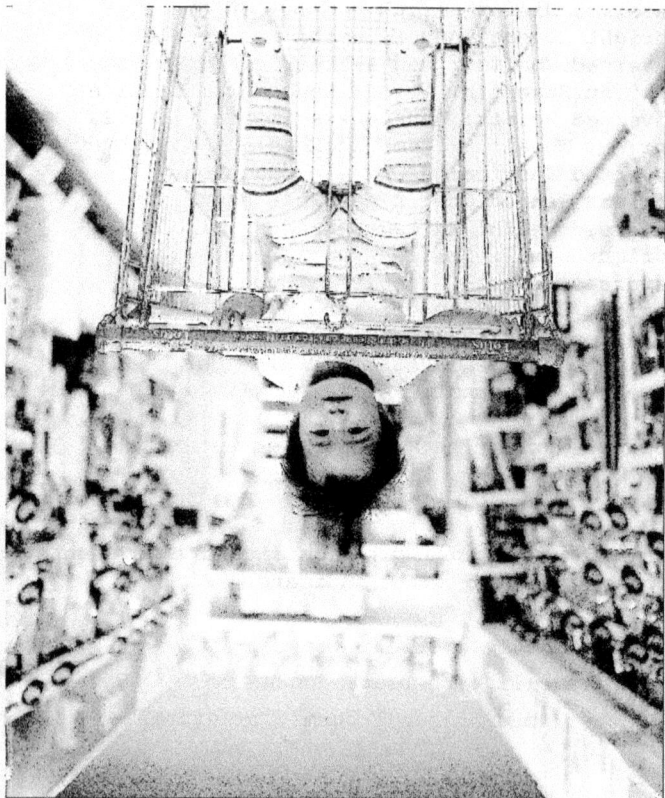

XV

Devil is attachment, self-victimization, and
addiction. The baby is trapped, surrounded by
material desires, and unsure of what to do.

XV
The Devil Reversed

Upright, the Devil is indicative of addictions, greed, violence, and learned helplessness. There is a compelling need to rid oneself of temptations and desires, but often the querant can not see a way out of the devastation in which they find themselves.

Reversed, there are often more positive interpretations of the upright card, but do be forewarned that it could be the upright meaning even more intensified.

Figure out which interpretation might apply to your situation:

1. Breaking free of restraint or addiction
2. Reclaiming personal power
3. Detachment or avoidance
4. Doom, collapse, illness, or destruction
5. Finding balance between light and dark

Questions answered by the reversed Devil:

Who? Someone who has recently broken free
What? Natural items
Where? The Earth; a farm
When? December to January; planting season; the harvest
Why? "As soon as we left the ground, I knew I had to fly." ~Amelia Earhart
Yes or No? Not until you free yourself

The Devil reversed
Before any card: Breaking free from (card)
After any card: Rehabilitation; independence

The Devil reversed as:

...an action?
- Break out of your shell
- Write a letter
- Quit your terrible job

...a place in your house?
- The library
- The kitchen
- The dining room
- Your bed

...a place in your city?
- A rehab center
- A nonprofit organization
- A family restaurant

...a place in the world?
- A theme park
- Finland
- Iceland
- Former Spanish or Portuguese colonies

...something to eat?
- Organic foods
- Superfoods like açai, blueberries, etc

...something to clean?
- The hammock or resting space
- The bookshelf
- A bedroom

...where to find the missing item?
- On the bookshelf
- Where you were last sitting down

...a color? Dark blue

...a movie theme? Breaking free, rehabilitation
- 28 Days
- Accepted
- Forgetting Sarah Marshall

...a new career?
- Addictions counselor
- Recruiter
- Tour guide
- Finish your post-secondary degree

Possible Major Arcana combinations with The Devil reversed:

Reversed Fool: Carefree abandon
Upright Magician: Manifestation of desires
Reversed Priestess: Breaking free of emotional blackmail or a difficult emotional period
Upright Empress: Nature; fertility; harvest
Reversed Emperor: Breaking free of tyranny
Upright Hierophant: An ethical decision
Reversed Lovers: An amicable divorce
Upright Chariot: A protest; bucking trends
Reversed Strength: Freedom brings insecurity
Upright Hermit: One knows what they need to do
Reversed Wheel: Trying to recover from a string of bad luck
Upright Justice: Clarity in confusing times
Reversed Hanged One: Fear of freedom
Upright Death: Rehab; preventing death
Reversed Temperance: Taking freedom to excess
Upright Tower: A shocking and surprising (usually positive) end to a serious problem
Reversed Star: Too shaken up to love
Upright Moon: Freedom is only an idea or dream
Reversed Sun: A difficult end to partnership
Upright Judgement: A new beginning; freedom
Reversed World: A delay to independence; immigration problems

The Major Arcana represent significant life events. The Devil reversed could indicate:

- Going to rehab or AA
- Release from imprisonment
- The end of a bad relationship
- Gaining independence

Hey, how'd you guys break free of my badass chains?

I dunno, she did it. You comin' babe?

Nah, we're over too

The Tower

XVI

The Tower upright is disaster or chaos.
Reversed, there are a few meanings including
fear, avoiding disaster, or even worse chaos!

XVI
The Tower Reversed

Upright, the Tower is strongly associated with catastrophic end. It is a card of sudden and unexpected shock, chaos, and disruption. There is perhaps tragedy associated with this card, such as a deadly natural disaster, an unexpected revelation, or the devastating end of a relationship

A card of such universal devastation means that when reversed it's hard to narrow down the meaning to a few quick ideas, but here are a few options:

1. Avoiding the upright disaster
2. A very personal transformation or tragedy
3. The fear of change or catastrophe
4. An oppression or inability to free oneself

Questions answered by The reversed Tower:

> **Who?** A difficult person; one who has recently suffered a catastrophe
> **What?** Cleanup after a storm or emergency
> **Where?** A volatile location; an area after a storm
> **When?** March to April, October to November; After the tragedy
> **Why?** "Times of crisis, of disruption or constructive change, are not only predictable, but desirable. They mean growth. Taking a new step, uttering a new word, is what people fear most." - Fyodor Dostoevsky
> **Yes or No?** No

The Tower reversed
> **Before any card:** Recovery from a disaster related to (card theme)
> **After any card:** Disaster recovery

The Tower reversed as:

...an action?
- Visit a therapist for grief or recovery
- Take a long, hot bath to relax
- Cry it out

...a place in your house?
- The peephole
- The window in the front door
- The tub
- The liquor cabinet

...a place in your city?
- A recently dismantled building
- A place with "Tower" in the title
- A rehab, recovery, or grief counseling location

...a place in the world?
- New Zealand
- The Caribbean
- A global humanitarian aid foundation

...something to eat?
- Canned goods
- Granola or trail mix
- Peanut butter

...something to clean?
- Prepare or replenish emergency supplies
- Throw out 16 dangerous pieces of clutter

...where to find the missing item?
- Near a fire hazard or dangerous item

...a color? Electric blue

...movie theme? Disaster recovery; fear of ruin
- Bird Box
- Thor: Ragnarok

...a new career?
- Disaster recovery
- Nonprofit humanitarian work
- Grief counseling or psychotherapy

Possible Major Arcana combinations with The Tower reversed:

> **Upright Fool:** Keep an eye on the kids
> **Reversed Magician:** Fear of job loss
> **Upright Priestess:** Personal trouble; emotions
> **Reversed Empress:** A worried mother or parent
> **Upright Emperor:** A struggling business
> **Reversed Hierophant:** A falling out; lost faith
> **Upright Lovers:** Avoiding a breakup; no divorce
> **Reversed Chariot:** Fear of flight; travel delayed
> **Upright Strength:** Training for emergencies
> **Reversed Hermit:** Lack of adequate preparation
> **Upright Wheel:** Disaster avoided this time
> **Reversed Justice:** White collar crime
> **Upright Hanged One:** decisions must be made to avoid disaster, don't delay
> **Reversed Death:** Unnecessary fear
> **Upright Temperance:** Everything is in balance
> **Reversed Devil:** Smooth sailing; all disasters are averted
> **Upright Star:** Foretells recovery from disaster
> **Reversed Moon:** A difficult journey to recovery
> **Upright Sun:** After a big change there is bliss
> **Reversed Judgement:** Extreme self-doubt
> **Upright World:** A personal transformation

The Major Arcana represent significant life events. The Tower reversed could indicate:

- Disaster recovery
- Cleanup after a natural catastrophe
- Fear
- Reconciliation

What fire? It's all good. Don't mind the tape.

The Star

XVII

The Star is about hope and healing. Reversed,
it is despair, illness, and disappointment.
The baby's world is flipped upside down.

XVII
The Star Reversed

Upright, the Star is a card of hope, faith, and inspiration. After the destruction of the tower card comes a bright future, positive changes, wealth and happiness.

Reversed, imagine one's world completely flipped upside down by a preceding tragedy. All hope is lost, and all that can be felt is failure and devastation. The Star, whether upright or reversed, cautions us to continue having hope.

Here are a few other things that could be happening. Figure out which one is correct for you:

1. Despair
2. A personal rejection
3. Focusing only on the negatives
4. A terrible event leaves one with no hope

Questions answered by The Star reversed:

Who? A "Debbie Downer"; a negative person
What? A bad accident
Where? Inland; a dirty place
When? January to February; during a meteor storm; a cloudy evening
Why? "You can't win unless you learn how to lose." ~Kareem Abdul-Jabbar
Yes or No? Maybe

The reversed Star
Before any card: Despair and hopelessness about (card)
After any card: Loss; illness; faithlessness

The Star reversed as:
...an action?
- Rest and wait
- Create a to-do list
- Stop asking questions of the Tarot

...a place in your house?
- The bathroom
- The chore list
- A spill

...a place in your city?
- A pile of rocks
- A yoga studio
- A law office
- A water park

...a place in the world?
- Hong Kong
- Denver, Colorado
- Hollywood, CA
- Somalia

...something to eat?
- Fried Rice
- Taro
- Corn
- Soybeans

...something to clean?
- The floors
- The TV and media room
- The shower

...where to find the missing item?
- Under the sofa
- In the bathroom
- They fell on the floor
- The windowsill

...a color? Gray, dull, orange, matte finish

...a movie theme? Despair, loss, falling stars
- A Star is Born
- Wall-E
- Gravity

...a new career?
- Teacher or professor
- Agent
- Public service

Possible Major Arcana combinations with The Star reversed:

> **Reversed Fool:** Being taken advantage of
> **Upright Magician:** Talented but insecure; shy
> **Reversed Priestess:** Repressing one's emotions
> **Upright Empress:** An unhealthy parent
> **Reversed Emperor:** A dictator
> **Upright Hierophant:** Losing faith in the church
> **Reversed Lovers:** A loss of trust in each other
> **Upright Chariot:** A spontaneous road trip
> **Reversed Strength:** Illness
> **Upright Hermit:** A need to plan next steps
> **Reversed Wheel:** Writer's block; no creativity
> **Upright Justice:** Justice will be delayed
> **Reversed Hanged One:** A test of wills
> **Upright Death:** A slow healing process
> **Reversed Temperance:** Lack of purpose and hope
> **Upright Devil:** Abuse; faithlessness
> **Reversed Tower:** Fear
> **Upright Moon:** Discouraging thoughts; self abuse
> **Reversed Sun:** Negativity; hopelessness
> **Upright Judgement:** Getting one's just desserts
> **Reversed World:** No closure after disappointment

The Major Arcana represent significant life events. The Star reversed could indicate:

- Despair
- Hopelessness
- Boredom
- A literal falling star; meteor shower

All hope is lost, Bird. Please just leave me here to wither away and die.

That's dramatic.

The Moon

XVIII

The Moon reversed might release anxiety and
fear, but it could be self-deceit or insomnia.
The upside-down moon is up to interpretation.

XVIII
The Moon

Upright, the Moon encapsulates the word *foreboding*. It indicates a difficult journey that must be taken to move forward in one's life. There may be deception, hidden dangers, or confusion along the way.

Reversed, the Moon is one of those tricky cards where there are could be a few different ways to interpret it, both positive and negative. The meanings will depend on who is asking and what the question is about.

Figure out what might be correct for you:

1. The release of fear and anxiety
2. Small problems; minor issues
3. A period of action; a *good* journey
4. A time for hope and renewal

Questions answered by The Moon reversed:

Who? The active one; the most honest person
What? A minor issue; an easy decision to make
Where? Beside a lake; where the moon reflects
When? During a full moon; during a new moon; late June to July; summer solstice; daytime
Why? "You don't have to see the whole staircase, just take the first step." ~Martin Luther King
Yes or No? Probably yes

The reversed Moon
Before any card: Your fears about (card) are unfounded
After any card: Resolution; the end of anxiety

The Moon reversed as:

...an action?
- Stop lying to yourself
- Take a risk

...a place in your house?
- The windows
- The kitchen cabinets
- The brightest room

...a place in your city?
- The river
- A seafood restaurant
- The park
- A forest

...a place in the world?
- Námafjall, Iceland
- Australia
- Alberta & Saskatchewan, Canada

...something to eat?
- Peanuts
- Lobster

...something to clean?
- The first thing you see when you look up
- The clutter on the staircase

...where to find the missing item?
- In plain sight
- Where the sun shines brightest

...a color? Orange, white

...a movie theme? Releasing fear, self-deceit
- Dune
- Finding Nemo
- Life of Pi

...a new career?
- Daycare provider
- Criminal
- Outdoor work

Possible Major Arcana combinations with The Moon reversed:

Upright Fool: Unwarranted fear of new things
Reversed Magician: Confusion; misrepresentation
Upright Priestess: Questioning oneself
Reversed Empress: Overwhelming anxiety
Upright Emperor: Overcoming business obstacles
Reversed Hierophant: Unconventional tactics
Upright Lovers: Misguided fear about the relationship – everything is fine
Reversed Chariot: Obstacles are in one's way
Upright Strength: Training for a dangerous job
Reversed Hermit: Blocked intuition; ignorance
Upright Wheel: Time brings an end to confusion
Reversed Justice: A misinterpretation of facts
Upright Hanged One: Release fear and just do it
Reversed Death: Focusing on minor problems
Upright Temperance: Getting help for anxiety
Reversed Devil: Finally breaking bad habits
Upright Tower: Small problem becomes a big one
Reversed Star: Discouragement; insomnia
Upright Sun: Freedom, success after trials
Reversed Judgement: No need to doubt a choice
Upright World: Trusting one's intuition

The Major Arcana represent significant life events. The Moon reversed could indicate:

- A period of confusion
- A bunch of little problems compounding
- Finding safety; the end of issues
- A new moon; a lunar eclipse

Look puppies, it's a *happy* moon!

The Sun

XIX

The Sun reversed is still joy, success, and
positivity, you may just be having trouble
viewing the sun through some pesky clouds.

XIX
The Sun

The Sun is the happiest card in the deck, regardless of whether it's upright or reversed. Upright, it means joy, positivity, freedom, success, fun, and any other positive word you can think of in your native tongue. The sun is a wonderful card to pull.

Even in a reversed position, the interpretation still promises that the sun will rise again soon. In most decks, the imagery on this card depicts excitement, joy and play.

With this card in a reading, even the most ominous fortunes have positivity and enlightenment in them, but the querant may not be able to see it. Reversed, here are some things that might be happening when this card is reversed:

1. Unhappiness; lack of enthusiasm
2. Unrealistic expectations
3. Pessimism; depression
4. Success after a difficult period

Questions answered by The Sun reversed:

> **Who?** A temporarily sad person; The least enthusiastic group member
> **What?** A small success; optimism
> **Where?** A shady spot
> **When?** July-August; a partly cloudy day; the vernal equinox; decent weather
> **Why?** "If only we'd stop trying to be happy we could have a pretty good time." ~Edith Wharton
> **Yes or No?** Yes, after a few minor issues

The reversed Sun
> **Before any card:** Unrealistic expectations about (card)
> **After any card:** Sadness, pessimism, ego

The Sun reversed as:

...an action?
- Cheer up
- Get more involved in achieving goals

...a place in your house?
- A well-lit room
- A comfy chair
- Where the children do schoolwork

...a place in your city?
- The hospital
- A viewpoint
- The zoo or theme park

...a place in the world?
- Hawaii, USA
- Oceania; the south pacific
- The Land of the Midnight Sun (Far North or South, depending on season)

...something to eat?
- Sun-baked foods
- Edible flowers
- Three square meals

...something to clean?
- The front or back porch
- Change broken lightbulbs

...where to find the missing item?
- In a well-lit room

...a color? Purple, blue, red

...a movie theme? Sadness, trying, no enthusiasm
- The Upside
- Still Alice
- Annie

...a new career?
- Dog walker
- Librarian
- Park ranger; horticulturalist
- Writer; freelancer

Possible Major Arcana combinations with The Sun reversed:

Reversed Fool: No confidence in new beginning
Upright Magician: One needs to get started
Reversed Priestess: Slowly coming around to an idea
Upright Empress: Postpartum depression
Reversed Emperor: Disappointing career
Upright Hierophant: Obligatory church visit
Reversed Lovers: A breakup
Upright Chariot: Don't put the cart before the horse
Reversed Strength: Many small obstacles ahead
Upright Hermit: Work or knowledge difficulties
Reversed Wheel: The future is unknowable at this time
Upright Justice: A difficult truth to hear
Reversed Hanged One: Stagnation is sadness
Upright Death: An upsetting change
Reversed Temperance: Mental illness
Upright Devil: An addictive personality
Reversed Tower: Suffering and negativity
Upright Star: Hope after sadness
Reversed Moon: Misinterpretation of situations
Upright Judgement: Closure after some delay
Reversed World: An incomplete project

The Major Arcana represent significant life events. The Sun reversed could indicate:

- Good times after a delay
- The sun will come out tomorrow
- A partly cloudy day

Cheer up, love. It's just a few clouds. The sun will come up tomorrow.

Judgement

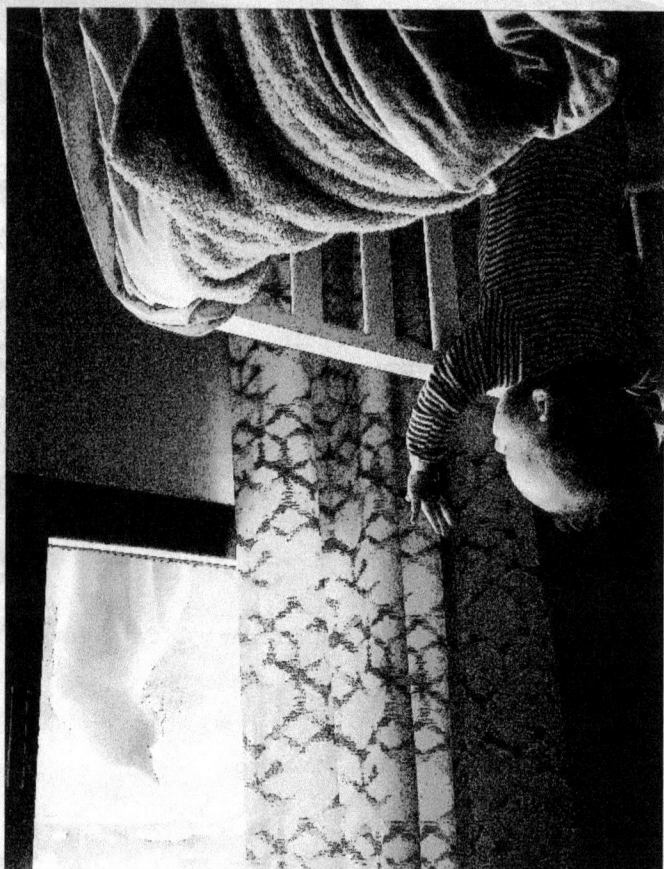

XX

Judgement is awakening and finding your
purpose. Reversed, it is self-doubt and not
living up to your potential.

XX
Judgement

AUTHOR NOTE: The word *Judgement* can be spelled with or without an E between the G and the M. Neither is more correct or more incorrect than the other, although for education's sake the 'e' is used more in British English and without the e is typically American English. I will flip-flop at random.

Whether upright or reversed, Judgement is a destiny card. A judgement of your life is a calculation of all the karma you have acquired, the good you have done, and the choices you have made. This defines your life's purpose and destiny.

Reversed, there are a few things that could be happening here. Figure out which one is correct for you:

1. Not living up to your purpose
2. Self-doubt
3. Being judgmental
4. Giving up possessions

Questions answered by Judgement reversed:

Who? The indecisive one
What? A missed opportunity
Where? Where the test takes place
When? No firm astrological dates; During the worst times; Stormy weather
Why? "Self-doubt kills talent." ~Edie McClurg
Yes or No? No

reversed Judgment
Before any card: Doubts surrounding (card)
After any card: Bad karma; lessons not learned

Judgement reversed as:

...an action?
- Turn off the TV
- Go camping
- Listen to your inner voice
- Write your ideas down

...a place in your house?
- A notepad
- The desk
- The TV

...a place in your city?
- A night club
- A funeral home
- The theatre
- A concert hall

...a place in the world?
- France
- The South Pacific
- Gibraltar
- China

...something to eat?
- Meat
- Mexican food
- Clean, raw food

...something to clean?
- The place you spend the most time

...where to find the missing item?
- Under a blanket

...a color? White; gray

...a movie theme? Self-doubt; bad movies
- Finding Dory
- Julie & Julia
- Almost any film in the DC franchise

...a new career?
- Advisor
- Consultant
- Parent
- Lawyer

Possible Major Arcana combinations with Judgement reversed:

> **Upright Fool:** Extreme doubt about a new start
> **Reversed Magician:** Inability to find purpose
> **Upright Priestess:** Self doubt
> **Reversed Empress:** Bad parenting choices
> **Upright Emperor:** An audit
> **Reversed Hierophant:** Misdirected blame
> **Upright Lovers:** Couple's counseling
> **Reversed Chariot:** Lost in the wilderness
> **Upright Strength:** One needs a personal trainer
> **Reversed Hermit:** Unwillingness to learn
> **Upright Wheel:** Cycles of self-loathing
> **Reversed Justice:** A very judgmental person
> **Upright Hanged One:** Indecisiveness
> **Reversed Death:** Change is necessary to move on
> **Upright Temperance:** Karma
> **Reversed Devil:** Regrets
> **Upright Tower:** A terrible illness
> **Reversed Star:** No hope; a lost cause
> **Upright Moon:** A difficult journey; rough water
> **Reversed Sun:** Severe mental illness & depression
> **Upright World:** Closure with regrets

The Major Arcana represent significant life events. Judgement reversed could indicate:

- Missing out on one's life purpose
- Bad karma
- Indecisiveness; lack of self-awareness
- Being too judgmental

You guys aren't living up to your purpose.

It's her fault.

Who, us? whaat? No

The World

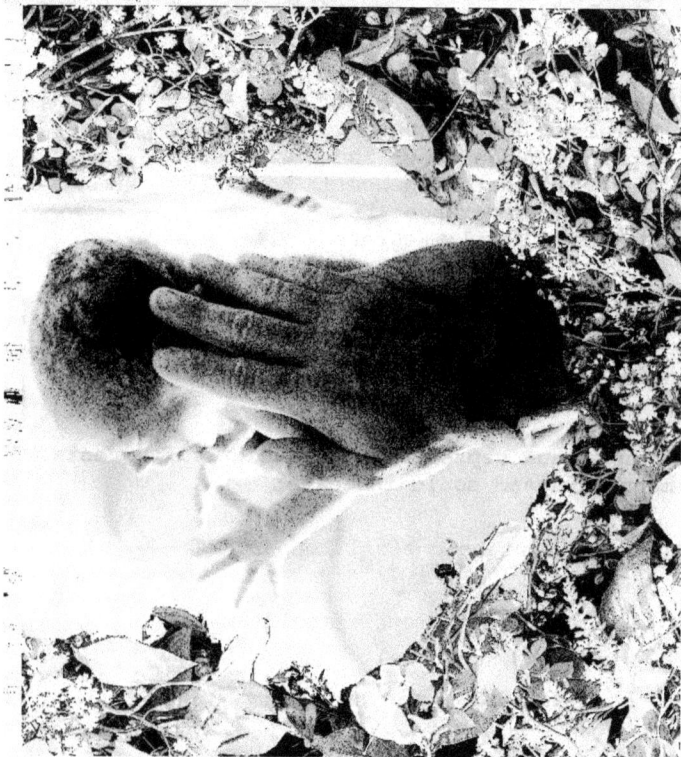

XXI

The World upright is success and fulfillment.
Reversed, nothing is complete yet. The
possibilities are still endless, just delayed.

XXI
The World Reversed

The World upright is achievement, completion, and feeling whole. It could be the end of a significant journey in one's lifetime, and the rewards were fulfilling and successful.

When the World card is reversed, it often means that completion is within reach, but there is something standing in the way. One might have stalled in their work right before the big reveal, such as a writer getting writer's block, or a musician quitting before their big break.

There are a few other reversed meanings that might be happening here:

1. Incomplete projects
2. Personal disappointments or stagnation
3. Heavy burdens
4. Pursuing a different path

Questions answered by The World reversed:

> **Who?** A person unable to move on
> **What?** Nothing; unfinished projects
> **Where?** Nowhere; a place of stagnation
> **When?** The end of the year; Capricorn; during delays
> **Why?** "Ten years from now, make sure you can say that you chose your life, you didn't settle for it." ~Unknown
> **Yes or No?** No; possibly, after work is done

The reversed World
> **Before any card:** Delays and issues with (card)
> **After any card:** Delays; immigration; problems

The World reversed as:

...an action?
- Start a project you'll never finish
- Quit your job
- Get off the internet

...a place in your house?
- The basement or garage
- An empty room

...a place in your city?
- The landfill
- A workshop
- A school

...a place in the world?
- Nowhere
- La Sagrada Familia, Barcelona; another of the world's most famous unfinished buildings

...something to eat?
- Pho
- Lasagna
- Jambalaya
- Rice pudding

...something to clean?
- Nothing - take a day off cleaning

...where to find the missing item?
- They're gone forever
- Near an unfinished project
- Under the globe or atlas
- On the floor

...a color? no color or all colors

...a movie theme? Incompletion, immigration
- District 9
- Elysium
- The Sun is Also a Star

...a new career?
- Postal service worker
- Civil service worker
- A job in another country
- Ambassador

Possible Major Arcana combinations with The World reversed:

Reversed Fool: No travel; trip cancelled
Upright Magician: A lazy but skilled worker
Reversed Priestess: Minor issues cause huge doubts
Upright Empress: Achievement causes ongoing problems
Reversed Emperor: Personal issues or baggage
Upright Hierophant: Immigration woes
Reversed Lovers: Acrimonious divorce
Upright Chariot: Running on fumes; trip delays
Reversed Strength: Insecurities; unmet goals
Upright Hermit: Finishing a project alone
Reversed Wheel: No end in sight to projects
Upright Justice: Justice does not bring closure
Reversed Hanged One: Querant is at fault
Upright Death: Finished project is incomplete
Reversed Temperance: Stroke; imbalance
Upright Devil: A difficult child
Reversed Tower: Paperwork or business problems
Upright Star: Unjustified worries
Reversed Moon: defection; exile; quitting
Upright Judgement: A misunderstanding

The Major Arcana represent significant life events. The World reversed could indicate:

- A disappointing ending
- No closure after years of hard work
- Immigration; a new country

To be honest, I just don't feel like working today.

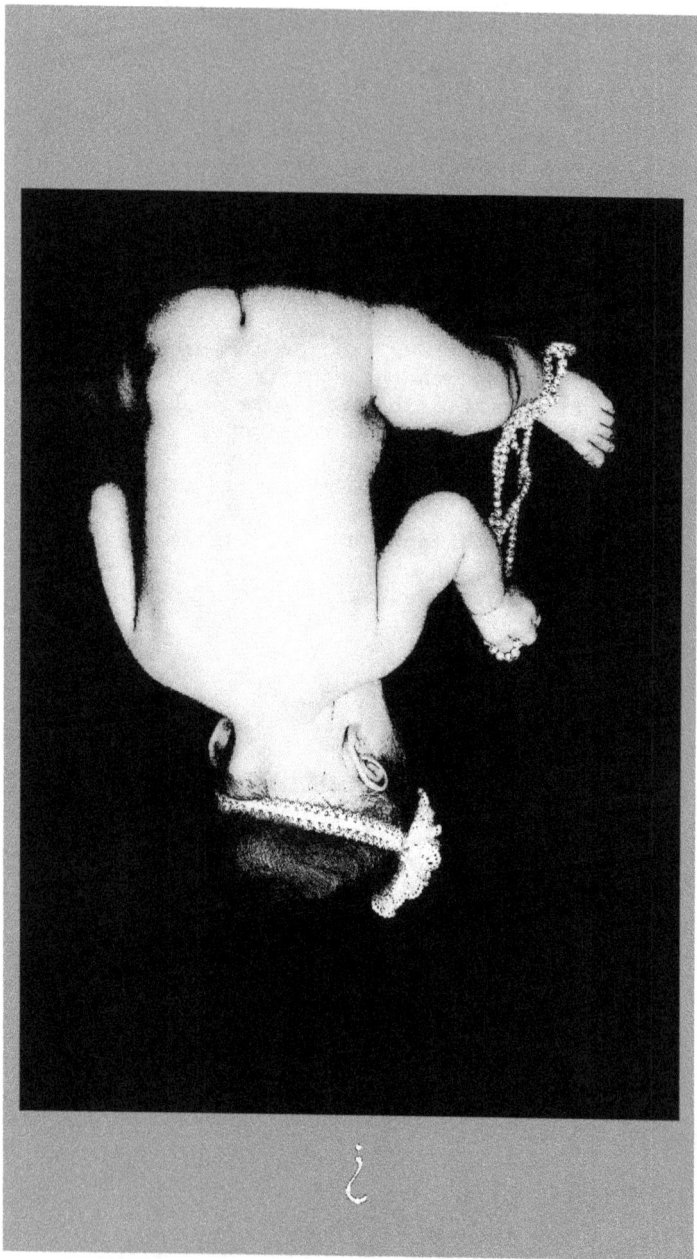

¿

Unless otherwise stated in your deck's manual,
this card is the same upright or reversed.

?
The 79th Card Reversed

Some Tarot decks have one or more extra Major Arcana cards. Often these are ultimate question cards, or have other specific names such as Gratitude, Artistry, or Ascension. Occasionally, you'll forget to remove a junk card before shuffling a new deck, and it will come up in a reading. You can use that as the 79th card.

Reversed, unless detailed in the book that comes with particular deck, it has similar interpretations to upright, or it can be more personal, or more negative.

Who? Who do you think?
What? What do you think?
Where? Wherever
When? Maybe never
Why? "We live in the world our questions create" ~David Cooperrider
How: You figure it out
Yes or No? Maybe!
An action? Think more about your situation
Place in your house, city, or world? Yes!
Looking for a job, food, color? Keep looking!
Movie? Something you're ambivalent about watching - you might be surprised
What should I clean? Whatever you'd like
Where are my keys? Unknown

79th Card reversed combinations:

Any combination with this card turns the answer back into a question.
For example, if you asked "what career should I look into" and pulled the Hierophant and the 79th card, your conscious mind might jump in and say "I love church! I could work there!" but ponder it a bit - you might realize you'd come to hate church if you were forced to attend it for work. The 79th card asks you to think about it.

¿

The Minor Arcana
Reversed

What are the Minor Arcana?

The Minor Arcana, also known as the Pips or the Lesser Arcana, are the suit cards. In most decks, they are depicted as wands (or clubs), cups (hearts), swords (spades) and pentacles (diamonds, coins, or disks).

Where the Major Arcana represent huge life-altering events that cannot be radically altered, the Minor Arcana might be people, events, or other everyday goings-on that are mutable and variable. The Minors represent events the querent can affect by changing something about their daily schedule or life.

When reversed, there are a myriad of ways to interpret the Minors, but here's a very rough guide:

- Wands represent air, our instincts, and our career and business. When reversed, it is generally the negatives of these institutions.

- Cups represent water, emotions, and our relationships and love life. When reversed, it is generally overreaction, breakups and the like.

- Swords represent fire, knowledge, and the internal conflicts we have in our own minds. When reversed, they're about philosophy, thought, and are generally positive.

- Pentacles represent earth, money, and the physical and material world that we can see and touch, rather than the instinctual or spiritual world. When reversed, they are generally about greed and materialism.

The 52 cards of a typical playing card deck can also be used as pip cards, either for divine and nebulous fortune telling, or for the purposes here - simplistic answers to everyday questions.

Sentence Combinations Calculator

I have created a table of words using some of the most rudimentary interpretations from each Reversed Minor Arcana card.

In the real world of Tarot, each card presents a variety of meanings based on different contexts, such as the question being asked, the person asking it, or the mood of the day. So absolutely feel free to replace these words with your own interpretations as you see fit.

If you own the upright book, *Applied Tarot*, you can see that these reversed interpretations aren't always just antonyms of the upright terms. Often, they are the worst facets of the upright interpretations. There are some exact antonyms in these reversed combinations, but not many.

You can use the following words in any combination and in any structure of phrase. When I ask a question, I typically pick three cards. As each card is drawn, I order them:

Verb > Adjective > Noun

Some prepositions you could add between the cards are: about, with, of, at, through, for, regarding, by, etc.

Wands Reversed

	Verb	Adjective	Noun
Ace	Copy	Uninspiring	Endings
Two	Ignore	Unprepared	Apprehension
Three	Impede	Apprehensive	Limits
Four	Disagree	Stifling	Opposition
Five	Yield	Combative	Compromise
Six	Fail	Egotistic	Disgrace
Seven	Give up	Powerless	Weakness
Eight	Slow	Stagnant	Exhaustion
Nine	Doubt	Vulnerable	Paranoia
Ten	Procrastinate	Unmanageable	Relief
Page	Demotivate	Temperamental	Secrets
Knight	Split	Arrogant	Inaction
Queen	Destroy	Cruel	Busybody
King	Discourage	Inexperienced	Rage

Cups Reversed

	Verb	Adjective	Noun
Ace	Deny	Sad	Insincerity
Two	Separate	Unequal	Breakup
Three	Criticize	Unsupportive	Enemies
Four	Focus	Boring	Unease
Five	Overcome	Healing	Acceptance
Six	Release	Uncreative	Baggage
Seven	Question	Clear	Reality
Eight	Cling	Missing	Search
Nine	Discourage	Superficial	Misery
Ten	Isolate	Unstable	Dysfunction
Page	Obsess	Vindictive	Envy
Knight	Idolize	Troublemaking	Moodiness
Queen	Discriminate	Insecure	Smotherer
King	Withdraw	Immature	Cheater

Swords Reversed

	Verb	Adjective	Noun
Ace	Confuse	Misunderstood	Lies
Two	Coerce	Illogical	Stalemate
Three	Forgive	Optimistic	Reconciliation
Four	Awaken	Restless	Burnout
Five	Settle	Resentful	Resolution
Six	Forget	Confined	Entrapment
Seven	Distrust	Regretful	Guilt
Eight	Escape	Empowering	Freedom
Nine	Fear	Shadowy	Nightmares
Ten	Survive	Recovering	Regeneration
Page	Misunderstand	Delinquent	Cynic
Knight	Follow	Aggressive	Inferiority
Queen	Manipulate	Bitter	Pessimism
King	Intimidate	Controlling	Irrationality

Pentacles Reversed

	Verb	Adjective	Noun
Ace	Spend	Unfortunate	Insecurity
Two	Drop	Rigid	Losses
Three	Mistake	Uncooperative	Discord
Four	Control	Greedy	Instability
Five	Breakthrough	Plentiful	Improvement
Six	Take	Exploitative	Debts
Seven	Overlook	Unfinished	Laziness
Eight	Err	Unfulfilling	Mediocrity
Nine	Desire	Codependent	Dissatisfaction
Ten	Bankrupt	Unsuccessful	Exile
Page	Disregard	Disorganized	Clutter
Knight	Wait	Stubborn	Complacency
Queen	Neglect	Uncaring	Selfishness
King	Corrupt	Ruthless	Materialism

Just now I've asked, "What message does the Universe have for me today?" and I drew:

Reversed Four of Cups > Reversed Page of Pentacles > Reversed Nine of Wands

Using the combinations calculator in Verb/adjective/noun form, I get

Focus (on) Disorganized Paranoia

I know what that's about. I have repairpersons coming over today and there is clutter all over my kitchen. I need to stop writing (focus) and clean the mess (disorganized) so they don't think terrible things of me (paranoia.)

I guess I'll go do that.

A few more combinations are included in the card pages. They might expand on these super quick references, or they might show different ways the reversed and upright cards can be interpreted based on the situation.

Combining the Reversed Major Arcana

I do not typically include Major Arcana in simple word combos, as there is nothing simple about them – they have a fixed and unwavering meaning and represent a significant moment in your life. The Majors are not good at nitpicking the minutiae of everyday things.

However, do include the Major Arcana if you would like deeper interpretations, or if you just don't feel like separating them from the deck.

If you choose to include them, I recommend you read the Major Arcana as fixed nouns and change your sentence structure accordingly, rather than using them as adjectives and verbs.

The Major Arcana do not describe something else; they *are* the thing you need to know about.

I can't repeat this enough: **Always treat the Majors as nouns.** Here are some suggestions:

The Fool Reversed: Recklessness
The Magician Reversed: Manipulation
The High Priestess Reversed: Delusion
The Empress Reversed: Insecurity; Infertility
The Emperor Reversed: Vanity; The Patriarchy
The Hierophant Reversed: Rebellion
The Lovers Reversed: Conflict
The Chariot Reversed: Obstacles
Strength Reversed: Weakness
The Hermit Reversed: Loneliness
The Wheel of Fortune Reversed: Bad luck
Justice Reversed: Injustice
The Hanged Man Reversed: Martyrdom; Hypocrisy
Death Reversed: Stagnation
Temperance Reversed: Imbalance; Extremes
The Devil Reversed: Independence
The Tower Reversed: Rebuilding
The Star Reversed: Doubt
The Moon Reversed: Confusion
The Sun Reversed: Negativity
Judgement Reversed: Indecision; Regret
The World Reversed: Incompletion
The 79th card Reversed: Interrogation

For example, I've asked the cards "What major event do I need to expect today?" and pulled the Reversed Hierophant and the Reversed Empress, which mean "Rebellion" and "Insecurity."

I don't know what that means at this point, but it's early in the day so I guess I'll see what happens and update later.

Update: Three hours later, my kid called me in a panic because she was about to lose her new rental house over not having the right insurance (insecurity.) I called our insurer but the 24/7 callcenter person said "this isn't something we do over the phone after hours."

So we found a new insurer that does do it over the phone after hours, and we went with them (rebellion.)

The system works and the day is saved!

The Major Arcana are about these major events of existence - in my kid's case, she was about to lose a rental and be rendered homeless, so we had to scramble and figure out a new way to fix the problem. Reversed Tarot cards are often quite foreboding and negative, but if you release your fears about their slightly negative connotations and instead figure out what cautions they have for you, you can find positive ways to work with them.

As you draw cards, keep in mind that trying to ask a simple everyday question of the Major Arcana will often get you an answer that is far more overwhelming and often less fixable than you might hope for in a simple Tarot reading.

Now, go forth and...

Seven of Wands

Knight of Pentacles

Page of Swords

Verb:	Adjective:	Noun:
Quit	(your) **Stubborn**	**Cynicism**

Or be a cynic if you want, but you can still have some fun with the Reversed Tarot!

Wands *Reversed*

Wands represent fire, our instincts, or our career and business. When reversed, every Wand card has several different interpretations based on context, but they tend to be more negative interpretations of those themes.

Ace of Wands

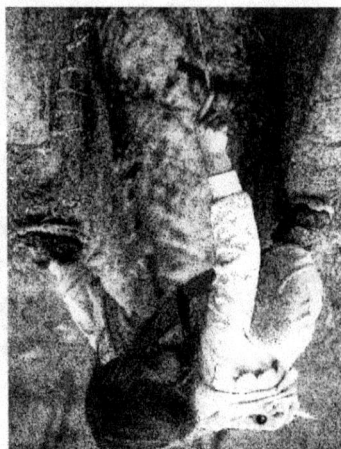

Ace of Wands Reversed

Upright, the Ace of Wands is the birth of a new career, a bright idea, a new project being launched, or the spark of creativity.

Reversed, these fresh starts are delayed, and there is frustration and impatience. One might have no energy or enthusiasm, or there is plenty of inspiration but the querant is not grabbing at the opportunity.

Questions answered by the reversed Ace of Wands:

> **Who?** An apathetic person; An arsonist
> **What?** A fire; A boring movie
> **Where?** A shack
> **When?** Later, now is not a good time. June through September, either the entire season of Summer (Northern Hemisphere) or Winter (Southern Hemisphere)
> **Why?** "The cure for boredom is curiosity. There is no cure for curiosity." ~Dorothy Parker
> **Yes or No?** No

The reversed Ace of Wands as:
...an action?
- Outline the small steps to take
- Direct your energy toward your goals
- Get started

...a place in your house?
- The copy machine
- A cluttered shelf

...a place in your city?
- The location of a famous fire
- The DMV

...a place in the world?
- The World Trade Center
- London, England
- Chicago
- Egypt

...something to eat?
- Cereal or granola
- Beer

...something to clean?
- A downstairs bathroom
- The fire pit

...where to find your missing item?
- Near wood or a fire
- In a boring place

...a color? Green

...a movie theme? Uninspired; failure
- Titanic
- Lucy
- Lost in Translation
- Little Miss Sunshine

...a new career?
- Data entry or paper pusher
- Virtual teacher or proctor
- Firefighter

The reversed Ace of Wands -
> **Before any card:** You've missed an opportunity for (card)
> **After any card:** Delays; bad news; creative blocks

Two of Wands

Two of Wands Reversed

The Two of Wands upright is the thoughtful planning before you commit to a project.

Reversed, there are a few interpretations for the Two of Wands. You may be feeling forced to make a decision too quickly. Alternatively, you're feeling stuck due to factors outside yourself. You may also have to go inward to do some personal development before you can take action.

Questions answered by the reversed Two of Wands:

Who? Someone unable to get started
What? An accident; a broken boat; indecision
Where? The lake
When? The last week of March; A couple of months wait
Why? "No one can hit their target with their eyes closed." ~ Paulo Coelho
Yes or No? No

The reversed Two of Wands as:
...an action?
- Give up and start again
- Wait

...a place in your house?
- The toilet
- A hallway
- The back door

...a place in your city?
- A dam
- The suburbs
- A boat or car repair shop

...a place in the world?
- Saskatchewan, Canada
- The Three Gorges Dam, China
- Kansas
- Russia

...something to eat?
- Ramen
- Rice

...something to clean?
- The bathroom

...where to find your missing item?
- In the sink
- You'll find them after a short wait

...a color? Black, green

...a movie theme? Bad planning; limited options
- Fyre (2019)
- The Wedding Planner
- Indiana Jones
- MacGyver (TV)

...a new career?
- Boat repair
- Coach
- Farmer

The reversed Two of Wands
    Before any card: a lack of options surrounding (card)
    After any card: Indecision; lack of planning; fear

Three of Wands

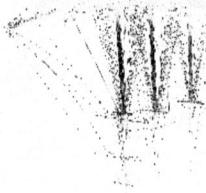

Three of Wands Reversed

The Three of Wands upright indicates a time where conditions are favorable for success. The Three of Wands says your ship will come in!

Reversed, several problems could have arisen that makes success seem less likely. You might have been too apprehensive to get started, you may lack planning and skills to move forward, or you might encounter too many obstacles and delays. Lastly, this card could indicate someone returning home after a long trip.

Questions answered by the reversed Three of Wands:

Who? Someone who is frustrated with a project
What? A broken boat; an unfinished project; delays
Where? Downtown; traffic
When? The first week of April; After a stressful delay
Why? "Delay is preferable to never." ~Danish proverb
Yes or No? It depends on the situation; after a wait

The reversed Three of Wands as:
...an action?
- Do more planning before you begin
- Seek help from others

...a place in your house?
- Your broken-down boat (*Bust Out Another Thousand*)
- The phone (call for help!)

...a place in your city?
- The valley
- The shipyard
- A large ugly building

...a place in the world?
- Alang Beach, India
- Rotherhithe, England
- Brownsville, Texas

...something to eat?
- Chips
- Milk

...Something to clean?
- The entryway
- Mop the floors

...where to find your missing item?
- With the firewood

...a color? Green, red, turquoise

...a movie theme? Delays; obstacles
- The Princess Bride
- Waiting for Godot; Waiting for Guffman
- Into the Wild

...a new career?
- Boat repair
- City or urban planner

The reversed Three of Wands
Before any card: Cooperation is needed for (card)
After any card: Delays; Lack of planning

Four of Wands

Four of Wands Reversed

The Four of Wands upright is joy, community, and togetherness.

Reversed, there are blocks or troubles surrounding one's home environment, routines may be stifled, the home may be unhappy, or something is unstable.

Questions answered by the reversed Four of Wands:

> **Who?** An ungrateful person
> **What?** A broken home
> **Where?** Outside the house
> **When?** Mid-April; Not until the issues are resolved
> **Why?** "To save your business, your job, your career, your relationship and your marriage. Choose to over communicate rather than not to communicate at all." ~DJ Kyos
> **Yes or No?** Resolve issues before asking again

The reversed Four of Wands as:

...an action?
- Resolve a dispute
- Say thank you

...a place in your house?
- In the yard

...a place in your city?
- A shelter
- A cutthroat workplace

...a place in the world?
- The Silk Road
- Cuba
- Russia

...something to eat?
- A TV dinner
- A meal for one

...something to clean?
- The front steps; outside the front door
- The baseboards

...where to find your missing item?
- Outside
- On the floor

...a color? Green, dark blue; dark gray

...a movie theme? Communication problems; transients
- Dumplin'
- The Pursuit of Happyness

...a new career?
- Family therapist
- Plumbing; electrical; home repair person
- Builder; construction
- Phone operator

The reversed Four of Wands
> **Before any card:** Communication breakdown around (card)
> **After any card:** Family conflicts; a broken phone

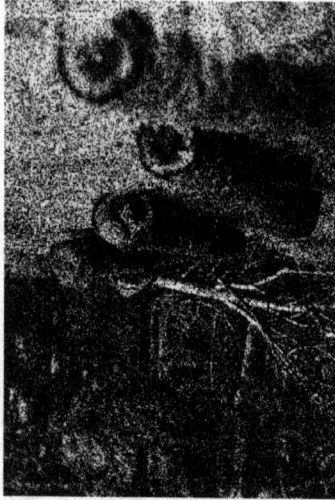

Five of Wands

Five of Wands Reversed

The Five of Wands is one of the particularly
difficult cards to interpret, both upright and reversed.
It depends on the context and the question asked.

When upright, it's possible a conflict has arisen
or may happen soon. Reversed, this card could indicate
compromise or finding a solution to that conflict, but
it could also imply battle fatigue – where the
disagreement is unwinnable and the querant just wants to
be done already.

Questions answered by the reversed Five of Wands:

Who? A shy person; an athlete who is frequently
benched
What? A cancelled sports game
Where? Home base; An empty sports field
When? July 21-30; When the disagreement stops
Why? "The gem cannot be polished without
friction, nor man perfected without trials."
~Chinese Proverb
Yes or No? No

The reversed Five of Wands as:

...an action?
- Cancel a sports game
- Sit this one out

...a place in your house?
- The sofa
- The den

...a place in your city?
- An empty arena
- A hotel
- A cosmetics or perfume shop

...a place in the world?
- Tokyo, Japan
- The location of cancelled Olympic games
- Berlin, Germany

...something to eat?
- Saltines
- Avocado toast
- Sweet potatoes

...something to clean?
- Blood
- Sports equipment
- Shred paperwork from old jobs

...where to find your missing item?
- Under the bed
- Near unused sports equipment

...a color? Green, orange, crimson

...a movie theme? After a fight; desperation
- The Bourne Identity
- The Imitation Game
- Reality competitions (TV)

A new career?
- Sales
- Management consultant
- Zoologist; park ranger; other work with animals

The reversed Five of Wands
  Before any card: Make a compromise about (card)
  After any card: Conflict; solutions

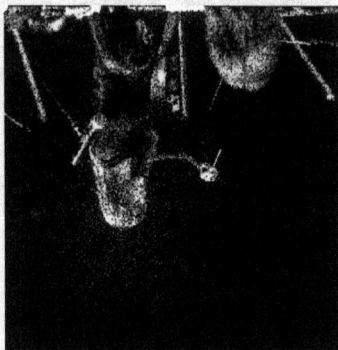

Six of Wands

Six of Wands Reversed

Upright, the Six of Wands is the card of victory, success, and recognition from others.

Reversed, it often means a failure to achieve success, or not receiving the accolades one believes they deserve. It could indicate hot-headedness and frustration as well.

Questions answered by the reversed Six of Wands:

Who? The loser of the game
What? A cancelled awards ceremony
Where? A dive bar
When? First week of August; After a loss
Why? "There's nothing wrong with being a loser, it just depends on how good you are at it."
~Billie Joe Armstrong
Yes or No? Maybe later

The reversed Six of Wands as:

...an action?
- Change your plans
- Accept defeat

...a place in your house?
- A cluttered surface
- The TV
- The kitchen after a party

...a place in your city?
- A war memorial
- A pub
- The local losing team's arena

...a place in the world?
- Phoenix, AZ
- Tampa Bay, FL
- Bulgaria
- Greece

...something to eat?
- Carbs
- Salad

...something to clean?
- The closets
- Soot

...where to find your missing item?
- Where you were last disappointed with yourself

...a color? Green, purple, magenta

...a movie theme? Losers; underdogs
- Bring It On
- Cool Runnings

...a new career?
- Casino dealer
- Social worker or victim advocate

The reversed Six of Wands
> **Before any card:** Unsuccessful (card)
> **After any card:** Failure, delay

Seven of Wands

Seven of Wands Reversed

Upright, the Seven of Wands is about standing up for your beliefs and defending what matters most to you.

Reversed, this card could mean giving up, giving in, admitting defeat, or feeling too overwhelmed to take any action in a difficult situation.

Questions answered by the reversed Seven of Wands:

Who? The overwhelmed person
What? A losing battle; a waste of time
Where? A debate; a meeting
When? The middle of August; After defeat
Why? "There's always some relief in giving up."
~Lauren Oliver
Yes or No? No

The reversed Seven of Wands as:

...an action?
- Stop arguing; surrender
- Change your thinking; learn something new

...a place in your house?
- The dining room
- The bathroom

...a place in your city?
- An arena for the losing team
- An ex-employer's office

...a place in the world?
- Finland
- Alcatraz prison, CA
- Ordos, China
- Jerusalem

...something to eat?
- Alcohol
- Smoothie

...something to clean?
- Sweep the floor
- The basement stairs

...where to find your missing item?
- Where you last gave up looking for it
- On the floor near your shoes

...a color? Orange, indigo

...a movie theme? Giving up; changing beliefs
- Legally Blonde
- An Inconvenient Truth
- 13th

...a new career?
- Something you are overqualified for
- Self-help book author
- Customer support advocate

The reversed Seven of Wands
> **Before any card:** Give up on (card)
> **After any card:** Powerlessness; an unwinnable battle

Eight of Wands

Eight of Wands Reversed

Upright, the Eight of Wands indicates swift energy, action, or travel overseas.

Reversed, this card is usually about rushing or moving too fast without taking appropriate steps. You may also be exhausted, anxious, or insecure. The eight of wands is often a warning to slow down and drive carefully.

Questions answered by the reversed Eight of Wands:

Who? An ER doctor or nurse
What? A fast-approaching deadline
Where? Downtown
When? The end of November; Immediately
Why? "Nature does not hurry, yet everything is accomplished." ~Lao Tzu
Yes or No? No

The reversed Eight of Wands as:

...an action?
- Drive slowly
- Work on plans, not action

...a place in your house?
- The car
- The dining room table

...a place in your city?
- A restaurant
- A shopping mall
- A park bench
- A busy intersection

...a place in the world?
- Costa Rica
- Italy
- Okinawa, Japan

...something to eat?
- Nuts and fruit
- Buttery meals

...something to clean?
- The bathtub
- Dust light fixtures or ceiling fans
- The trunk of the car

...where to find your missing item?
- In the glove compartment
- At eye level, such as on a shelf or cabinet

...a color? Orange, red

...a movie theme? Rushing around; mental confusion
- Rush Hour
- Speed
- John Wick
- Memento

...a new career?
- Airport baggage handler
- Tour guide
- Barista or bartender

The reversed Eight of Wands
Before any card: Missing details about (card)
After any card: Mental confusion; insecurity

Nine of Wands

Nine of Wands Reversed

The Nine of Wands upright is about finding one's inner strength during an ongoing battle.

Reversed, the battle still rages but the querant might be stubborn or unwilling to learn lessons about it. Alternatively, one might just be exhausted and lack the courage required to persist.

Questions answered by the reversed Nine of Wands:

Who? The most stubborn person
What? A stalemate
Where? A fenced off area
When? The first week of December; When you've learned your lesson; After a failed attempt
Why? "Sometimes in life, your situation will keep repeating itself until you learn your lesson." ~Brigitte Nicole
Yes or No? No

The reversed Nine of Wands as:

...an action?
- Learn from your mistakes
- Tear down the broken fence or door
- Take a nap

...a place in your house?
- The fence or the walls
- A room you haven't visited in awhile

...a place in your city?
- A hospital
- A hotel
- Jail

...a place in the world?
- Venezuela
- South Asia
- Scandinavia

...something to eat?
- Soup
- Avocado

...something to clean?
- Stubborn stains
- The toilet

...where to find your missing item?
- In the bathroom

...a color? Purple, red

...a movie theme? Stubbornness; exhaustion
- The Lion King
- Birdman or (The Unexpected Virtue of Ignorance)
- Clerks

...a new career?
- Journalism
- Rescue worker

The reversed Nine of Wands
> **Before any card:** Learn your lesson about (card)
> **After any card:** Exhaustion; inflexibility

126

Ten of Wands

Ten of Wands Reversed

The Ten of Wands upright is about overburdening ourselves and working too hard.

Reversed, there are a few things that might be happening with the huge amount of work you have to do:

1. You could be taking on too much
2. You might be avoiding your responsibilities
3. You may be beating a dead horse

Questions answered by the reversed Ten of Wands:

Who? The most overworked person
What? Wrong priorities
Where? The office or workplace
When? The middle of December; Never; When you start doing the work you're putting off
Why? "Some people believe holding on and hanging in there are signs of great strength. However, there are times when it takes much more strength to know when to let go and then do it." ~Ann Landers
Yes or No? Yes, if you do the right work

The reversed Ten of Wands as:

...an action?
- Ask for help
- Give up

...a place in your house?
- The laundry room
- The garage

...a place in your city?
- A storage facility
- An industrial park
- City Hall

...a place in the world?
- Hong Kong
- The East coast of USA
- Tokyo, Japan

...something to eat?
- Duck pâté
- Pot roast
- Baked Alaska

...something to clean?
- The laundry room
- The kid's room

...where to find your missing item?
- In a pile of laundry

...a movie theme? Martyrdom; overburdened
- Limitless
- The Intern

...a new career?
- Healthcare worker
- Oil rig or iron worker
- Busy, irrelevant work

The reversed Ten of Wands
> **Before any card:** Share the workload of (card)
> **After any card:** Unfinished work; burnout

Page of Wands

Page of Wands Reversed

The Page of Wands upright foretells of news regarding something creative, innovative, or entrepreneurial.

Reversed, this news might be bad, fake, or fearful. Alternatively, the querant might be acting impatiently, procrastinating, or becoming gullible to a situation.

Questions answered by the reversed Page of Wands:

Who? A liar
What? Bad news
Where? A daycare or preschool
When? Summertime (Northern Hemisphere) or Winter (Southern Hemisphere); During a boring period; soon
Why? "Both optimists and pessimists contribute to society. The optimist invents the aeroplane, the pessimist the parachute." ~George Bernard Shaw
Yes or No? No

The reversed Page of Wands as:

...an action?
- Find a distraction; procrastinate
- Play a new game

...a place in your house?
- The pile of bills
- Blank sheets of paper

...a place in your city?
- A coffee shop
- A movie theatre

...a place in the world?
- Japan
- Taiwan
- Australia
- Texas

...something to eat?
- A chocolate orange
- dried fruit
- Beef

...something to clean?
- The junk mail
- The hallway

...where to find your missing item?
- The bathroom
- With the recycling

...a color? Green, blue, purple

...a movie theme? Bad news; pessimism
- The Social Dilemma
- Run Lola Run

...a new career?
- Editing
- Quality Control

The reversed Page of Wands
> **Before any card:** Bad news about (card)
> **After any card:** Procrastination; fraud

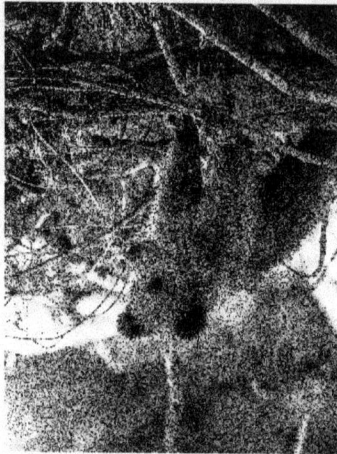

Knight of Wands

Knight of Wands Reversed

The Knight of Wands upright grows bored easily and values new adventure over common sense.

Reversed, these traits are often magnified to dangerous levels. This person could be arrogant, reckless, loud, or obnoxious. Alternatively, they may be so fearful they are unwilling to do anything at all.

Questions answered by the reversed Knight of Wands:

Who? A daredevil
What? A cancelled trip
Where? A loud party
When? Mid July to mid-August; Quickly and recklessly
Why? "There are two circumstances that lead to arrogance: one is when you're wrong and you can't face it; the other is when you're right and nobody else can face it." ~ Criss Jami
Yes or No? No, in most situations

The reversed Knight of Wands as:

...an action?
- Drink coffee or tea
- Think things through

...a place in your house?
- Your work desk
- The stove

...a place in your city?
- An outdoor activity center, such as skydiving
- The racetrack
- A car dealership

...a place in the world?
- The ocean
- Australian outback
- Caminito del Rey, Spain

...something to eat?
- Coffee
- Puffer fish
- The Carolina reaper pepper

...something to clean?
- The outside windows
- The backseat of the car
- Hiking or camping gear

...where to find your missing item?
- A display case or shelf
- In plain sight
- In the car

...a movie theme? Arrogance; recklessness
- Bridesmaids
- Guardians of the Galaxy

...a new career?
- Private chef
- C-suite executive; director

The reversed Knight of Wands
Before any card: An ambitious person shows off (card)
After any card: Arrogance; daredevil activity.

Queen of Wands

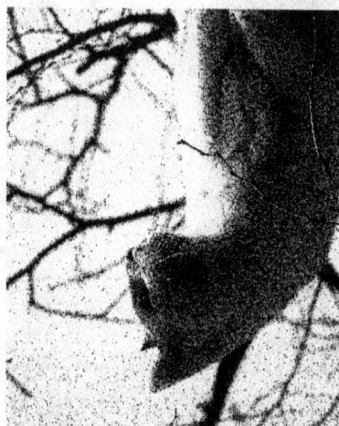

Queen of Wands Reversed

The Queen of Wands upright represents extroversion, beauty and friendliness. The queen is self-reliant and successful through their own merits.

Reversed, the queen might be demanding, manipulative, or have low self-esteem and be a busybody.

Questions answered by the reversed Queen of Wands:

Who? A nosy busybody
What? Unmet demands
Where? The home of a cheater
When? March and April; in a few months
Why? "There was nothing more dangerous than people convinced of their own good intentions." ~Laura Lippman
Yes or No? Maybe

The reversed Queen of Wands as:

...an action?
- Apologize for your actions
- Find positivity and gratitude

...a place in your house?
- The front window
- The kitchen

...a place in your city?
- A café
- An assisted living facility
- A pet store

...a place in the world?
- Latin America
- One's city of birth
- Portugal
- The Philippines

...something to eat?
- Tea
- Juice
- Pastries and cakes

...something to clean?
- The sitting room

...where to find the missing item?
- Near the coffee machine or kettle

...a color? Green, brown

...a movie theme? Manipulation; jealousy
- Gone Girl
- Murder on the Orient Express

A new career?
- Recruitment or HR
- Nutritionist or disease prevention

The reversed Queen of Wands
> **Before any card:** Someone is deceitful about (card)
> **After any card:** Manipulation; nosiness; jealousy

King of Wands

King of Wands Reversed

Upright, the King of Wands is a powerful and commanding community leader who is optimistic and devoted.

Reversed, someone might be acting inauthentically, or be impulsive, abusive, or disloyal.

Questions answered by the reversed King of Wands:

Who? A tyrant
What? A broken promise
Where? A courtroom; a boxing ring
When? August or November; soon
Why? "I had finally begun to grasp something that should have been immediately apparent: that someone had opposed the great march toward equality; someone had been the person from whom freedom had to be wrested." ~Tara Westover
Yes or No? Yes, but not easily and manipulation is involved

The reversed King of Wands as:

...an action?
- Accept help without demands
- Change your plans

...a place in your house?
- A full-length mirror
- A vanity

...a place in your city?
- A lucrative business
- A political office

...a place in the world?
- France
- China

...something to eat?
- Imported liquor
- An expensive cut of meat
- Burgers and hot dogs

...something to clean?
- The bathroom vanity or cabinets

...where to find your missing item?
- The closet
- The bathroom counter

...a color? Red, yellow

...a movie theme? Disloyalty; betrayal
- The Empire Strikes Back
- Harry Potter and the Deathly Hallows

...a new career?
- The entertainment industry
- Law
- I.T.

The reversed King of Wands
> **Before any card:** A misalignment of values about (card)
> **After any card:** rage; selfishness

Cups *Reversed*

Cups represent water, emotions, and our relationships and love life. When reversed, every Cups card has several different interpretations based on context, but they tend to involve negative and overreactive emotions.

Ace of Cups

Ace of Cups Reversed

The Ace of Cups upright tells us to trust our emotions, start a new relationship, or open ourselves up to joyful messages from the Universe.

Reversed, our feelings may be blocked, our heart may be too guarded to let love and light in, or we might be going through a breakup, an affair, or fertility issues.

Questions answered by the reversed Ace of Cups:

> **Who?** Someone cold and distant; a cheater
> **What?** A miscarriage; spilled milk
> **Where?** At a party you didn't want to attend
> **When?** Soon; The entire season of Fall (Northern Hemisphere) or Spring (Southern Hemisphere); After a spill
> **Why?** "You never lose by loving. You always lose by holding back." ~ Anonymous
> **Yes or No?** No

The reversed Ace of Cups as:

...an action?
- Process your emotions
- Take a vacation by yourself
- Break up with your partner

...a place in your house?
- A leaky faucet
- The laundry room
- The dishwasher
- The glassware

...a place in your city?
- A sewage treatment facility

...a place in the world?
- Southeast Asia
- Venezuela
- Zacatón, Mexico
- Tuscany, Italy

...something to eat?
- Popcorn
- A tub of ice cream
- Booze
- Chocolate

...something to clean?
- The laundry
- The glassware
- Your eyeglasses

...where to find your missing item?
- Near a leak or spill

...a color? Blue, black, gray

...a movie theme? Longing; being alone
- The Fault in Our Stars
- Sideways
- Eternal Sunshine of the Spotless Mind

...a new career?
- Trades
- Network Administrator
- Engineer

The reversed Ace of Cups
    Before any card: A need to take a break from (card)
    After any card: Longing; sadness; loss

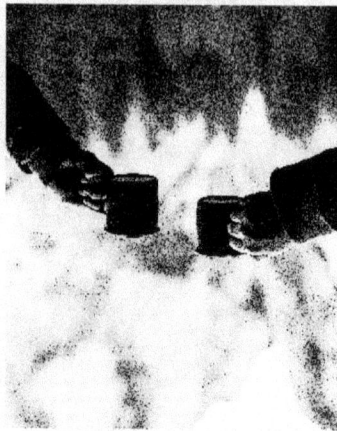

Two of Cups

Two of Cups Reversed

The Two of Cups upright is true companionship, and the card foretells of success in relationship, companionship, business, or friendship.

Reversed, there is disharmony in the relationship. The couple may be unhappy or going through a breakup, or a business partnership could be ending. At its worse, there is an imbalance of power leading to abuse or the end of a friendship.

Questions answered by the reversed Two of Cups:

Who? An ex-lover or former business partner
What? A breakup
Where? A bar
When? The last week of June; After the split.
Why? "Never regret. If it's good, it's wonderful. If it's bad, it's experience." ~Victoria Holt
Yes or No? Not until after a division

The reversed Two of Cups as:

...an action?
- Call your ex
- Go it alone

...a place in your house?
- The toilet
- A single statue
- A La-Z-Boy chair

...a place in your city?
- Divorce court
- A business under new management

...a place in the world?
- Reno, NV
- New York City
- Thailand
- Minneapolis, MN
- The Amazon

...something to eat?
- Cheetos
- Tacos

...something to clean?
- The shower

...where to find the missing item?
- In the bathroom
- The last person you were with took them

...a color? Orange, green

...a movie theme? Breaking up; dissolving a partnership
- Definitely, Maybe
- Joy
- Jerry Maguire

...a new career?
- Divorce attorney
- Mediator
- Private Investigator
- Auditor

The reversed Two of Cups
> **Before any card:** Disharmonious (card)
> **After any card:** Breakup; divorce

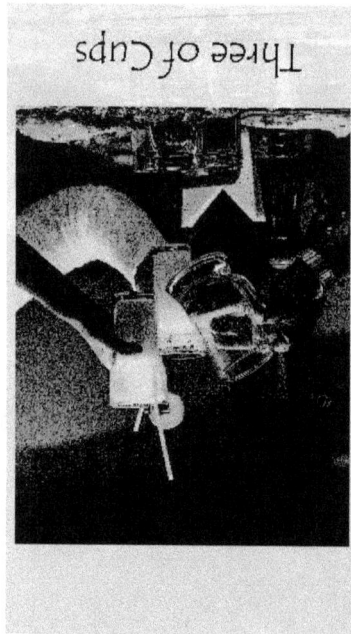

Three of Cups Reversed

Upright, the three of cups is about platonic love, community, and friendship.

Reversed, the friendships have gone sour. There may be peer pressure, gossip, or cancelled events. Alternatively, a partner might be having an affair, as in "three's a crowd," or a couple could have suffered a pregnancy loss.

Questions answered by the reversed Three of Cups:

Who? A mistress or affair partner; a gossip
What? A cancelled celebration
Where? An empty wedding venue; an overturned boat
When? The first week in July; Too soon
Why? "An insincere friend is more to be feared than a wild beast; a wild beast may wound your body, but an evil friend will wound your mind." ~Unknown
Yes or No? Maybe

The reversed Three of Cups as:

...an action?
- Cancel plans
- Quit drinking

...a place in your house?
- The toilet
- The dishwasher
- The fridge
- The recycling bin

...a place in your city?
- A brunch restaurant
- The café
- A golf course

...a place in the world?
- Thailand
- Italy
- Spain
- Germany

...something to eat?
- Tea
- Crumpets
- Liquor
- Leftovers

...a color? blue, gray, red

...a movie theme? Infidelity; gossip
- Promising Young Woman
- Crazy Rich Asians
- Love Actually

...a new career?
- Concierge
- Recruiter or HR

...something to clean?
- The liquor cabinet
- Your social media friends list

...where to find your missing item?
- In the front hall closet
- Under the table

The reversed Three of Cups
> **Before any card:** Plans cancelled because of (card)
> **After any card:** Gossip; an affair

Four of Cups

Four of Cups Reversed

Upright, the Four of Cups is boredom, fatigue and apathy.

Reversed, one is ready to seize opportunities but may be unsure of where to start. It is about letting go of regrets and finding gratitude for the little things. If you pull the reversed four of cups, be ready to wake up.

Questions answered by the reversed Four of Cups:

Who? Someone looking to find themselves again
What? A spirit quest
Where? On a mountain
When? The middle of July; When one is ready for a change
Why? "You will recognize your own path when you come upon it, because you will suddenly have all the energy and imagination you will ever need."
~Jerry Gillies
Yes or No? Maybe

The Four of Cups reversed as:

...an action?
- Go on a personal retreat
- Change something about your life
- Start a gratitude journal

...a place in your house?
- The porch, patio, or balcony
- The garden

...a place in your city?
- The hills
- A career counseling office

...a place in the world?
- Bali
- Iceland
- Switzerland

...something to eat?
- Yogurt
- Avocado toast
- Cheese platter

...something to clean?
- Don't clean today, do something fun instead

...where to find your missing item?
- Near the front door
- In the car

...a color? Red

...a movie theme? Finding yourself; awakening
- Amélie
- Chef
- Ratatouille

...a new career?
- Spirit guide
- Career counselor

The reversed Four of Cups
> **Before any card:** Seize an opportunity about (card)
> **After any card:** Enthusiasm; focus

Five of Cups

Five of Cups Reversed

The Five of Cups upright is regret or grief about something that happened in the past, and it's an indication that we should try to look forward and find the positives.

The Reversed five is this looking forward. It is moving on from defeat, letting go of sorrow and regrets, and doing our best to rejoin society after a setback.

Questions answered by the reversed Five of Cups:

Who? Someone moving forward
What? Letting go
Where? Ahead of you
When? The last week of October; 5 days or weeks from now; When you let go
Why? "You can spend minutes, hours, days, weeks, or even months over-analyzing a situation; trying to put the pieces together, justifying what could've, would've happened… or you can just leave the pieces on the floor and move on."
~Tupac Shakur
Yes or No? Maybe

The reversed Five of Cups as:

...an action?
- Forgive
- Start a gratitude journal
- Take a break from your relationship

...a place in your house?
- The cabinet
- Luggage storage

...a place in your city?
- The airport
- A pub with friends
- The suburbs

...a place in the world?
- The United States
- Russia
- The United Kingdom

...something to eat?
- Dried fruit
- Crackers and peanut butter

...something to clean?
- The area directly in front of you

...where to find the missing item?
- In front of you

...a color? White, brown

...a movie theme? Letting go; forgiveness
- Thor
- Zootopia
- Moonlight

...a new career?
- Dishwasher
- Delivery driver
- Flight attendant

The Five of Cups reversed
    Before any card: Letting go of (card)
    After any card: forgiveness; acceptance; better days ahead

Six of Cups

Six of Cups Reversed

Upright, the Six of Cups is about childhood, nostalgia, homesickness, and those old dreams that may no longer be realistic.

Reversed, the card indicates a maturity or growing up. It could represent someone moving out of the family home or letting go of a difficult past. In a negative sense it might also represent being bored or lacking that youthful spark of creativity

Questions answered by the reversed Six of Cups:

Who? A new adult; a child moving out of the house
What? Broken toys; memories
Where? In a new location; away from home
When? The first week of November; In the recent past; When a child moves out
Why? "A ship does not sail with yesterday's wind." ~Louis L'Amour
Yes or No? Yes

The reversed Six of Cups as:

...an action?
- Do the mature thing
- Get married
- Buy a house
- Cooperate

...a place in your house?
- A stack of bills to pay
- The kitchen prep space

...a place in your city?
- The courthouse
- A continuing education center
- A real estate office

...a place in the world?
- The next biggest city
- A concert hall
- The DMV

...something to eat?
- Wine and cheese at a fancy restaurant
- Waffles
- Sliders

...something to clean?
- The office
- Scrub the pet litter box or kids' dirtiest toy

...where to find your missing item?
- Under a stack of paperwork

...a color? blue, green

...a movie theme? Maturing, empty nesting
- Lady Bird
- Pleasantville
- Bao

...a new career?
- Working with new adults or college graduates
- Archaeologist
- Social worker

The reversed Six of Cups
> **Before any card:** Letting go of (card)
> **After any card:** maturity, leaving the nest

Seven of Cups

Seven of Cups Reversed

Upright, the Seven of Cups could be high hopes, wishful thinking, or in a practical sense it's a set of options to choose from.

Reversed, it could be a lack of decent choices, or a reality check in a difficult situation.

Questions answered by Seven of Cups reversed:

Who? A sober person
What? Clarity
Where? Firmly on the ground; other side of the fence
When? The middle of November; When you wake up; Seven hours from now
Why? "Let us make our future now, and let us make our dreams tomorrow's reality." ~Malala Yousafzai
Yes or No? Yes

The reversed Seven of Cups as:

...an action?
- Ground yourself in reality
- Clean your glasses

...a place in your house?
- The workspace
- The toolbox
- Under the sink

...a place in your city?
- A public service building
- A transportation hub, like a bus or train station
- The office

...a place in the world?
- Mexico
- Shanghai
- Tokyo
- Russia
- Italy

...something to eat?
- Almonds
- Bananas
- Liquor
- Milk

...something to clean?
- The sink

...where are my keys?
- The last place you were working hard

...a color? red

...a movie theme? Grounding oneself in reality
- Groundhog Day
- Fantasia
- The Big Sick

...a new career?
- Psychotherapist
- Artist
- Nonprofit work

Seven of Cups reversed
> **Before any card:** Stay grounded about (card)
> **After any card:** reality, facts

Eight of Cups

Eight of Cups Reversed

The Eight of Cups upright might be someone going on a spirit quest, giving up on their current situation, or disillusioned with the present and ready to move on to the future.

Reversed, a few things could be happening. One might be afraid of commitment, they could be abandoning a person or situation without explanation, or they may lack emotional maturity or be partying too hard. Like it's upright counterparty, this eight needs to be interpreted in the moment.

Questions answered by reversed Eight of Cups:

Who? A youth
What? A cancelled event
Where? Far away
When? The end of February; When you've given up; When you walk away from your situation
Why? "At times in life you have to leave people where they left you." ~Angel Moreira
Yes or No? Maybe

The reversed Eight of Cups as:

...an action?
- Accept what you have
- Throw a party
- Run away

...a place in your house?
- The room you last walked out of

...a place in your city?
- A place to be alone
- A party store

...a place in the world?
- Alaska
- Ukraine
- Sonora, California
- The desert

...something to clean?
- The last thing you walked away from

...where to find the missing item?
- The last place you were
- You keep walking right by them

...something to eat?
- Stuffed mushrooms
- Mini meatballs

...a color? orange

...a movie theme? Avoidance or immaturity
- The Hangover
- The Incredibles

...a new career?
- Something completely different
- Retail work
- Camp counselor
- Tour guide

The reversed Eight of Cups
Before any card: Abandoning (card)
After any card: Immaturity; stagnation

Nine of Cups

Nine of Cups Reversed

Upright, the Nine of Cups is riches, luxury, and the satisfaction you receive from enjoying your wealth. It is sometimes a bit of smugness as well, or it could represent a shopkeeper who is ready to open their store to the world.

Reversed, the luxuries have been overturned or lost. It is misery, devastation, self-hatred and greed. Because cups are about emotions, it could also be a need for the end to a relationship, or a lack of joy.

Questions answered by the reversed Nine of Cups:

Who? An arrogant, disappointed person
What? A lack of fulfillment
Where? An uncomfortable place
When? The 1st week of March; 9 months after a loss
Why? "We must accept finite disappointment, but never lose infinite hope." ~Martin Luther King Jr
Yes or No? No

The reversed Nine of Cups as:

...an action?
- Take a break
- Show empathy for others
- Cheer up
- Close your shop

...a place in your house?
- A disappointing space

...a place in your city?
- A warehouse store
- A radio station
- A hospital or elder care center

...a place in the world?
- Loch Ness, Scotland
- Paris, France
- Casablanca, Morocco
- Las Vegas, Nevada

...something to eat?
- Boxed Mac & Cheese
- Club sandwiches
- Jell-o shots
- Pop tarts

...something to clean?
- The toilet
- The oven and fridge

...where to find your missing item?
- Near the trash

...a color? Blue

...a movie theme? Shattered dreams; unfulfillment
- American Beauty
- A Beautiful Mind
- Once Upon a Time in Hollywood

...a new career?
- Personal shopper
- IT
- Antique shopkeeper
- Two or more minimum wage jobs
- Part time work

The reversed Nine of Cups
Before any card: Disappointing and negative (card)
After any card: Failure; unhappiness

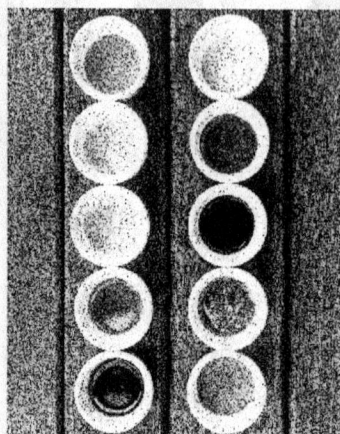

Ten of Cups

Ten of Cups Reversed

The Ten of Cups upright is about obtaining the
highest level of gratitude and emotional abundance. It
is reunions, gatherings, marriage, and harmony.

Reversed, the Ten of Cups might be a
dysfunctional family or broken home, or a lack of
security in one's marriage or housing. It sounds
terrible initially, but even reversed there is a
reminder to look around at all the things you can be
grateful for.

Questions answered by the reversed Ten of Cups:

Who? The dysfunctional family member
What? Disharmony
Where? A social services department
When? The middle of March; 10 months after a
divorce or broken home
Why? "Families are like fudge - mostly sweet with
a few nuts." ~Unknown
Yes or No? No

The Reversed Ten of Cups as:

...an action?
- Find things to be happy about
- Break up a difficult relationship
- Do not trust that person

...a place in your house?
- The half bath
- The kitchen sink

...a place in your city?
- Social services
- The DMV
- The school pickup line

...a place in the world?
- Reno, NV
- East Asia
- Seville, Spain
- Amsterdam

...something to eat?
- Bagged salad
- Takeout

...something to clean?
- The laundry
- Wipe the floors

...where to find the missing item?
- You lost it in a fight
- A parent or elder has it

...a color? Dysfunctional family
- Hillbilly Elegy
- Knives Out
- Parasite

...a new career?
- Divorce lawyer
- Child services
- Manual labor

The Ten of Cups reversed
>**Before any card:** A lack of security caused by (card)
>**After any card:** Unhappy home; dysfunction

Page of Cups

Page of Cups Reversed

Upright, the Page of Cups is creative and kind, possibly an artist or musician, who wants to be helpful but is a little shy about asking what you need from them.

Reversed, this young person may take their passion to the extreme and be obsessed and envious. Alternatively, they may have had his or her heart broken or have lost sight of their dreams.

Questions answered by reversed Page of Cups:

Who? A vindictive person
What? A sad event from the past
Where? A schoolyard
When? Autumn (Northern Hemisphere); Spring (Southern Hemisphere); in the past
Why? "Love is only made more valuable by the risk of heartbreak." ~Alessandra Torre
Yes or No? No

The Page of Cups reversed as:

...an action?
- Be careful
- Be selfish
- Go white-water rafting

...a place in your house?
- The elder's room
- A safe
- A spill

...a place in your city?
- An arid park
- An unromantic restaurant
- A gas station

...a place in the world?
- Iceland
- Thailand
- New Orleans
- Myanmar
- Venezuela

...something to eat?
- Couscous
- Shawarma
- Falafel
- Ostrich eggs

...something to clean?
- The floors

...where to find your missing item?
- In the bathroom
- Near broken or dirty dishes

...a color? Orange, green

...a movie theme? Envy; broken hearts
- Wonder Woman 1984
- Shazam
- Envy

A new career?
- Desk job for a large organization
- Seamstress
- Work at a seafood restaurant

The reversed Page of Cups
    Before any card: A creative block due to (card)
    After any card: Bad news; abuse

Knight of Cups

Knight of Cups Reversed

Upright, the Knight of Cups is confident in his drive and creativity, and is willing to jump into new and exciting adventures that might bring him more risk but could also lead to greater reward.

Reversed, this knight could be a heartbreaker, one prone to one-night-stands or suffering from unrequited love. Alternatively, there could be a revoked job offer, a creative block, or some type of disturbing event that makes this knight sad and moody.

Questions answered by reversed Knight of Cups:

Who? A person who didn't get the job
What? A broken promise
Where? On a hill
When? Mid-October to Mid-November; A missed moment
Why? "Do not pray for an easy life. Pray for the strength to endure a difficult one." ~Bruce Lee
Yes or No? No

The reversed Knight of Cups as:

...an action?
- Accept bad news with grace
- Don't jump to conclusion
- Revoke an offer

...a place in your house?
- A broken wall or door
- The single person's room

...a place in your city?
- The place you didn't get a job
- An antique shop
- A dive bar

...a place in the world?
- South Africa
- Stonehenge
- Japan
- Mexico

...something to eat?
- Water
- Liquor
- Soup
- Crabs

...something to clean?
- Your shoes
- The freezer

...where to find the missing item?
- Someone else has it
- Where you heard the bad news

...a color? yellow, dark grey

...a movie theme? Rejection; cheating
- Joker
- The Breaker Upperers
- Love, Actually

...a new career?
- Thief
- Thriller or suspense Novelist
- EMT

The reversed Knight of Cups
    Before any card: Bad news about (card)
    After any card: Cheating; rejection

Queen of Cups

Queen of Cups Reversed

The Queen of Cups upright is a virtuous and kind person, protecting all that they have with loyalty, intuition, and wisdom.

Reversed, this card could represent a treacherous or vindictive person, or someone who is insecure and needy. The thing to remember about this queen is that cups are all about emotions, so negative or smothering emotions are generally represented by the reversed card.

Questions answered by the reversed Queen of Cups:

Who? An enemy
What? Blocked creativity
Where? A field
When? Mid-June to Mid-July; Not any time soon
Why? "Sometimes our thoughts are backed with so much insecurity that they create lies we believe." ~Unknown
Yes or No? Uncertain

The Queen of Cups reversed as:

...an action?
- Calm down
- Call a friend
- Organize something

...a place in your house?
- A chair

...a place in your city?
- A pizza joint
- An ice cream truck

...a place in the world?
- Guatemala
- Finland
- Niagara Falls

...something to eat?
- Ice cream
- Fish sticks

...something to clean?
- The pantry
- Your saved pictures folder

...where to find the missing item?
- In the sink

...a color? Yellow; blue

...a movie theme? Insecurity, emotional manipulation
- Dumplin'
- Girl on the Train
- Gone Girl

A new career?
- Telemarketing
- Sales
- Singer

reversed Queen of Cups
> **Before any card:** Be cautious and reserved with (card)
> **After any card:** Insecurity; emotional manipulation

sdnɔ ɟo ƃuıʞ

King of Cups Reversed

Upright, the King of Cups is a mature person who leads with the heart, not the head. This King appreciates the finer things and is warm-hearted and calm.

Reversed, like the Queen, the King becomes emotionally immature, or overreactive. They may be anxious, uncaring, depressed, or withdrawn, or they might be a cheater.

Questions answered by the reversed King of Cups:

Who? An unbalanced male
What? An overreaction
Where? A stone monument
When? Mid-February to Mid-March; Mid October to Mid-November; when emotions are dealt with
Why? "Don't get mad. Don't get even. Do better. Much better. Rise above. Become so engulfed in your own success that you forget it ever happened." ~Unknown
Yes or No? No

The reversed King of Cups as:

...an action?
- Quit fantasizing and start doing
- Don't hide your emotions

...a place in your house?
- The backyard
- A room where you can be alone

...a place in your city?
- A theatre company
- A board room

...a place in the world?
- Russia
- Norway
- Madagascar
- Cambodia

...something to eat?
- Shrimp
- Cookies

...something to clean?
- Sweep the front porch
- Tune musical instruments

...where to find the missing item?
- Near rocks
- It fell from it's usual spot

...a color? Yellow; gray

...a movie theme? Immature male
- Hot Tub Time Machine
- Billy Madison
- Fight Club

...a new career?
- Dean
- Maintenance work
- Artist

The reversed King of Cups
> **Before any card:** Remain calm when confronted with (card)
> **After any card:** Anxiety; depression

Swords *Reversed*

Swords represent air, knowledge, and the internal conflict we have in our own mind. When reversed, they are the negative aspects of knowledge, however as most swords cards tend to be rather negative when upright, the reversed interpretations are sometimes surprisingly positive.

Ace of Swords Reversed

This upright Ace represents determination, intelligence, and focus. It may suggest a victory using the mind or one's wits.

Reversed, it's a lack of ideas or intelligence, hostility, misinformation, or possible memory loss. What are you forgetting?

Questions answered by the reversed Ace of Swords:

Who? The forgetful person
What? A failed exam or test
Where? Under the desk
When? An unknown time; December through March - The entire season of Winter (Northern Hemisphere) or Summer (Southern Hemisphere)
Why? "Forgetfulness is a form of freedom."
~Kahlil Gibran
Yes or No? Probably not

The reversed Ace of Swords as:

...an action?
- Remain patient during a problem
- Do a jigsaw puzzle

...a place in your house?
- The next room over
- Under a piece of furniture

...a place in your city?
- Elementary school
- The movie theatre
- A grassy knoll

...a place in the world?
- Mozambique
- Venezuela
- Nevada
- Texas

...something to eat?
- Fried foods
- Tuna on white bread

...something to clean?
- Sweep under the furniture

...where to find your missing item?
- The last place you felt stupid
- Under a large piece of furniture

...a color? Pantone 448 C "Drab dark brown"

...a movie theme? Ignorance; stupidity
- Idiocracy
- Dumb and dumber
- Zoolander

...a new career?
- I.T.
- Truck driver
- Plumber

The reversed Ace of Swords
> **Before any card:** A need to learn more about (card)
> **After any card:** Ignorance; memory loss

Two of Swords

Two of Swords Reversed

The upright Two of Swords may indicate a dilemma with no clear path forward, a decision with no right or wrong choice, or two paths - neither of which is better than the other.

When reversed, one is unable to make the decision needed to move beyond this two. It could be a postponement of a dream, the discovery of a lie, or some sort of unfair disadvantage when dealing with a choice.

Questions answered by the reversed Two of Swords:

Who? A liar
What? A delay
Where? A highway between two cities
When? The end of September; After a long delay; when a decision is reached
Why? "In any moment of decision, the best thing you can do is the right thing, the next best thing is the wrong thing, and the worst thing you can do is nothing." ~Theodore Roosevelt
Yes or No? No

The reversed Two of Swords as:

...an action?
- Be honest
- Make a decision
- Learn to juggle knives

...a place in your house?
- The knife drawer
- Heirloom swords
- A hallway with two directions

...a place in your city?
- A red light
- A meeting house
- A basketweave overpass

...a place in the world?
- A consulate or embassy
- Japan
- St. Maarten
- China
- India

...something to Eat?
- Korean food
- Asian fusion
- Seasonal fruits and vegetables

...something to clean?
- The silverware drawer
- The hallway

...where to find the missing item?
- Near the knives
- A dishonest person hid it from you

...a color? Beige or greige

...a movie theme? Stalemate; unfairness
- Mr & Mrs Smith
- 13th
- Keeping Up With The Joneses

...a new career?
- Lawyer
- Pastor
- Knife salesman
- Stay where you are

Two of Swords reversed
> **Before any card:** An unfair disadvantage due to (card)
> **After any card:** Delays; lies

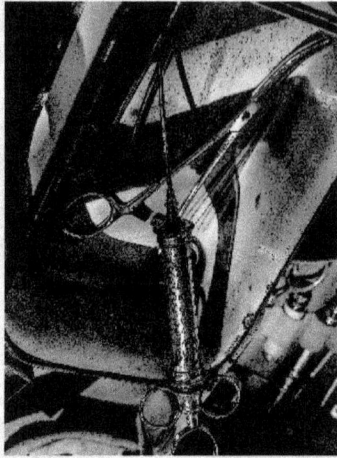

Three of Swords

Three of Swords Reversed

Upright, this three is a card of pain, heartbreak, and sorrow. It could be the end of a job or relationship, an accidental injury or death, or something else causing deep and difficult grief.

Reversed, the terrible events happened but we have overcome or started to overcome that pain. We can see the light at the end of the tunnel and are optimistic, reconciling differences, or trying to be positive.

Questions answered by reversed Three of Swords:

> **Who?** Long-divorced couple; an estranged friend
> **What?** The light at the end of the tunnel
> **Where?** A grief or support group
> **When?** The beginning of October; In the past; Three hours
> **Why?** "Even in the midst of devastation, something within us always points the way to freedom."
> ~Sharon Salzberg
> **Yes or No?** No

The Three of Swords reversed as:

...an action?
- Take all the time you need
- Ask for help
- Cancel something

...a place in your house?
- A shrine
- The back deck
- A fireplace
- The garage

...a place in your city?
- A recovery center
- Grief counseling
- An AA meeting
- Church

...a place in the world?
- Rwanda
- Japan
- British Virgin Islands

...something to eat?
- BRAT – Bananas, rice, apples, toast

...something to clean?
- The carpets
- Sweep the floor

...where to find the missing item?
- Where you last recovered it

...a color? Ombre, green

...a movie theme? Attempting to recover after devastation
- Kill Bill
- The First Wives Club
- Yesterday

...a new career?
- Recovery counselor
- Cleaning staff
- Construction

The reversed Three of Swords
> **Before any card:** Attempting to recover after (card)
> **After any card:** Recovery; forgiveness

Four of Swords

Four of Swords Reversed

The four of swords upright is about withdrawal and retreat, perhaps temporary, so you can recover.

Reversed, rest and recovery is slow or difficult. There may be burnout or a lack of proper self-care. Alternatively, it could be that moment after a decent rest, when we have the mental strength to fight again.

Questions answered by the reversed Four of Swords:

Who? An angsty or restless individual
What? A slow recovery
Where? A school; an office
When? The middle of October; Later; After a nap
Why? "Think what a better world it would be if we all, the whole world, had cookies and milk about three o'clock every afternoon and then lay down on our blankets for a nap." ~Barbara Jordan
Yes or No? Yes, but later

The reversed Four of Swords as:

...an action?
- Find stability
- Be prudent in your tasks

...a place in your house?
- The shower
- A comfy chair
- A bar

...a place in your city?
- A bar
- A recovery center
- An exercise studio
- A hair salon

...a place in the world?
- Atlanta, GA
- San Diego, CA
- India
- The Maldives

...something to eat?
- Coffee
- An energy drink
- Cucumber

...something to clean?
- Make the bed
- Your shoes

...where to find the missing item?
- By the front door

...a color? Blue; orange

...a movie theme? Awakening; burn-out
- Amelie
- Office Space
- I Heart Huckabees

...a new career?
- Freelance work
- Go back to school
- Construction

Four of Swords reversed
> **Before any card:** A recovery from (card)
> **After any card:** burn-out; lack of progress

Five of Swords

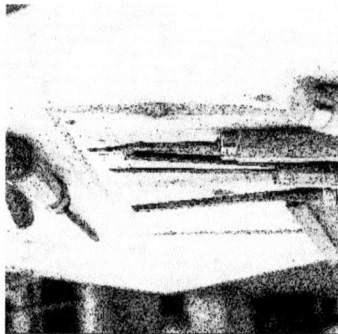

Five of Swords Reversed

Upright, the Five represents the time after a battle or conflict. If it is a victory, it is an empty one. If it's a defeat, it requires a major regroup and re-plan.

Reversed, this card is tricky because there are so many ways to look at it. If we imagine that it has the same meaning as the upright five but that the battle or conflict is ongoing inside ourselves, it becomes a bit easier. This card could mean compromise, sacrifice, or holding on to resentment.

Questions answered by reversed Five of Swords:

Who? Someone holding a grudge
What? The end of a conflict
Where? A place where a truce or mediation happened
When? The end of January; Five days after a fight
Why? "To be wronged is nothing, unless you continue to remember it." ~Confucius
Yes or No? No

The Five of Swords reversed as:

...an action?
- Forgive and forget
- Apologize

...a place in your house?
- The filing cabinet
- The dining table
- A video game system

...a place in your city?
- A law office
- An ice cream shop

...a place in the world?
- California, USA
- Taiwan
- Japan
- Germany

...something to eat?
- A box of chocolates
- A charceuterie board

...something to clean?
- Dishware
- Your room

...where to find the missing item?
- Where someone last apologized to you

...a color? Red, seafoam green

...a movie theme? Apologies, forgiveness
- Elf
- The Wedding Singer
- Three Billboards Outside of Ebbing, Missouri

...a new career?
- Lawyer or Law Clerk
- Designer
- Sales representative

The reversed Five of Swords
> **Before any card:** Holding a grudge about (card)
> **After any card:** Apologies, forgiveness

Six of Swords

Six of Swords Reversed

The Upright six depicts a gradual change or difficult journey. This is a troublesome trip, and one that is not wanted but is necessary for survival.

Reversed, someone is having trouble making that move forward. Perhaps there is a delay or cancellation of travel plans, someone has "rocked the boat" so to speak, or perhaps the worst has happened, such as a flood or a drowning.

Questions answered by the reversed Six of Swords:

>**Who?** A submissive person
>**What?** An inability to move
>**Where?** The water
>**When?** The first week in February; Six weeks ago
>**Why?** "Yesterday is not ours to recover, but tomorrow is ours to win or lose." ~Lyndon B. Johnson
>**Yes or No?** No

The Six of Swords reversed as:

...an action?
- Check the weather
- Listen to reason
- Stop fearing the unknown

...a place in your house?
- A shelf of memorabilia
- A plugged drain
- Dishwasher

...a place in your city?
- Your ex's apartment
- An old workplace
- The train station
- A freeway into town

...a place in the world?
- Southern USA
- Croatia
- Poland
- France

...something to eat?
- Comfort food
- Chicken nuggets

...something to clean?
- A closet
- The tub
- The boat

...where to find the missing item?
- It's right near you

...a color? Yellow, amber, red

...a movie theme? An inability to move on; trapped
- Eternal Sunshine of the Spotless Mind
- John Wick
- Jurassic Park

...a new career?
- Factory work
- Warehouse employee
- Remote work
- Caretaker

The reversed Six of Swords
Before any card: An inability to move on from (card)
After any card: Slow progress, travel delays

Seʌen ɟo Sᴚoᴚqs

Seven of Swords Reversed

The Seven of Swords upright is about stealth,
manipulation, and getting away with something sneaky.

Reversed, we're compelled to confess our sins,
turn over a new leaf, or we've been caught in a lie.
Alternatively, we might dig even deeper into the
sneakiness and become a pathological liar, a cheat, or
malicious

.

Questions answered by the reversed Seven of Swords:

Who? A pathological liar
What? A lie
Where? In your own home
When? The middle of February; After seven
confessions; after seven lies
Why? "When a lie is uttered, it naturally brings
with it more lies. It is an art, a form of
fiction writing." ~Chaker Khazaal
Yes or No? No

The reversed Seven of Swords as:

...an action?
- Face the consequences
- Do the right thing
- Confess

...a place in your house?
- The warning light in the car
- The fire alarms

...a place in your city?
- Church
- A casino

...a place in the world?
- Vatican City
- Machu Picchu

...something to eat?
- Fish
- Bread

...something to clean?
- Screens, such as on a cellphone, laptop, or TV

...where to find the missing item?
- Near your phone
- Under something to do with leaves (turning over a new leaf)

...a color? Purple; blush

...a movie theme? Confession, turning over a new leaf
- Despicable Me
- Aladdin
- Spider-Man: Far from Home

A new career?
- Pastor
- Something in a new city
- Consulting; training

Seven of Swords reversed
> **Before any card:** You're being dishonest about (card)
> **After any card:** Lies; confession

Eight of Swords

Eight of Swords Reversed

Upright, the Eight of Swords is about breaking free of self-victimization and finding your way out of a bad situation.

Reversed, this could be an incredibly positive card, where one has found their freedom and made an escape from whatever was holding them back. Alternatively, it could be a terribly negative interpretation of the upright card, where one has sunk deeper into despair or found that there is no way out of their situation.

Questions answered by the reversed Eight of Swords:

Who? Someone standing up to abuse
What? Facing your fears
Where? On the other side of the fence
When? The middle of May; When you are free
Why? "Fall seven times, stand up eight."
~Japanese proverb
Yes or No? Possibly

The reversed Eight of Swords as:

...an action?
- Find a solution
- Fix the gate
- Believe in yourself

...a place in your house?
- On the other side of the wall
- The playroom

...a place in your city?
- A park
- A car dealership
- A zoo
- A wide-open space

...a place in the world?
- Hadrian's Wall, UK
- Yosemite, CA
- Hveradalir, Iceland

...something to eat?
- Cheesecake
- Oatmeal
- Melting chocolate ball

...something to clean?
- Fingerprints off the walls
- The backs of chairs and doors

...where to find the missing item?
- Scattered across the room
- Standing upright in plain view

...a color? green, orange

...a movie theme? freedom, facing fears
- The Shawshank Redemption
- Django Unchained
- Wreck-It Ralph

...a new career?
- Construction
- Pilot
- Elevator technician

Eight of Swords reversed
>**Before any card:** Facing one's fear of (card)
>**After any card:** Escape, freedom

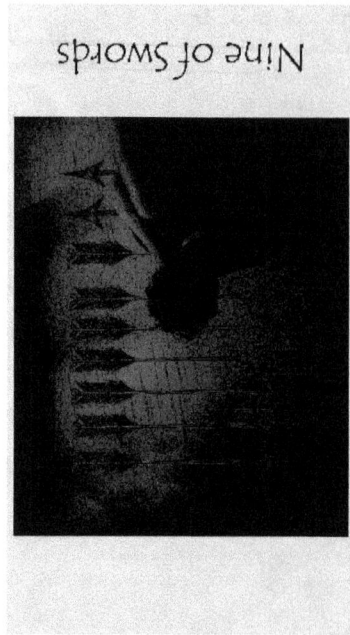

Nine of Swords

Nine of Swords Reversed

Upright, the Nine of Swords is a card of anxiety, pain, and nightmares.

Reversed, it is often about seeing the light at the end of a tunnel, being able to let go of some of the anxiety and negativity, and taking help when it is offered.

However, in rare instances it might be even worse than its upright meaning, and could represent extreme night terrors or a complete nervous breakdown.

Questions answered by the reversed Nine of Swords:

Who? A guilty person
What? A bad dream
Where? At the therapist's office; at recovery
When? The first week of June; When the light at the end of the tunnel becomes apparent; nine days
Why? "Cry. Forgive. Learn. Move on. Let your tears water the seeds of your future happiness." ~Steve Maraboli
Yes or No? No. Do not start serious things now

The reversed Nine of Swords as:
...an action?
- Practice coping mechanisms
- Accept or ask for help
- Write in a journal

...a place in your house?
- A chair in the bedroom
- The light in a dark closet

...a place in your city?
- A tunnel
- A bookstore
- A recovery center
- A self-help group

...a place in the world?
- The Portland Underground
- Montreal, Canada
- Wieliczka Salt Mine, Poland
- Spain

...something to eat?
- Salty food
- Coffee
- Tapas
- Honey

...something to clean?
- The attic
- A dark drawer or cabinet

...where to find the missing item?
- In your bed
- Under the furniture

...a color? White, Yellow

...a movie theme? Learning to cope; accepting help
- Groundhog Day
- The Incredibles

...a new career?
- Early shift work
- Tunnel or cave maintenance
- Psychoanalysis

The reversed Nine of Swords
> **Before any card:** Severe anxiety associated with (card)
> **After any card:** Nightmares, Being frightened

Ten of Swords

Ten of Swords Reversed

Upright, this Ten is pain, destruction, defeat, and a terrible end. There is nothing positive about this card. Even reversed, it can often represent clinging to disaster and not being able to move on.

However, there may also be some positives to the reversed interpretation. You could be rising above your difficulties, through the worst of a disaster, or your life could slowly be improving after a devastating event.

This is one Tarot card where the reversed interpretation might be better than the upright one.

Questions answered by reversed Ten of Swords:

Who? A survivor

What? An escape from disaster

Where? At the end of a long road or dark tunnel

When? The middle of June; After a devastation; ten days

Why? "Freedom is what we do with what is done to us." ~Jean-Paul Sartre

Yes or No? Yes

The reversed Ten of Swords as:

...an action?
- Fix something
- Celebrate your small accomplishments

...a place in your house?
- The toolbox
- The bathtub

...a place in your city?
- The river
- An event venue

...a place in the world?
- Switzerland
- Seattle, WA
- New Zealand

...something to eat?
- Vitamin C
- Berries, fruit, veggies, and nuts

...something to clean?
- Restock the first aid supplies
- The emergency prep storage

...where to find the missing item?
- On a tidy surface
- Someone else will find it for you

...a color? Rainbow; bright

...a movie theme? Recovering; surviving disaster
- Chef
- The Martian
- Stranger than Fiction

...a new career?
- Start a new business
- Knife salesman
- Chef
- Go back to school

The reversed Ten of Swords
Before any card: Surviving the worst of (card)
After any card: Regeneration; recovery

Page of Swords

Page of Swords Reversed

The Page of Swords upright heralds is the beginning of learning something new, or a fresh academic start. Although stubborn and intensely opinionated, the upright page is curious and intellectual.

Reversed, this page brings bad news, bad ideas, and a lack of education. They might be cynical, deceptive, or gossipy and opinionated.

Questions answered by reversed Page of Swords:

Who? A dimwit
What? gossip
Where? The coffee shop
When? The entire season of Winter (Northern Hemisphere), or Summer (Southern Hemisphere); When your head is in the clouds
Why? "Those who seek to know gossip will hear ill about themselves." ~Kate Morton
Yes or No? No

The reversed Page of Swords as:

...an action?
- Tell the truth
- Be wary of someone who may be taking advantage

...a place in your house?
- The internet router
- A whiteboard or message center

...a place in your city?
- The coffee shop
- The hair salon or barbershop

...a place in the world?
- Bolivia
- The Caribbean
- Portugal
- Cambodia

...something to eat?
- Hot tea
- Juicy fruit
- Turkey and stuffing

...something to clean?
- Teacups
- Coffee machine

...where to find the missing item?
- Near your coffee mug

...a color? Green

...a movie theme? Mental manipulation; gossip
- Inception
- Mean Girls
- Crazy Rich Asians
- In the Heights

...a new career?
- Communications and Informatics
- Private investigator
- Flight attendant

The reversed Page of Swords
> **Before any card:** Someone is being dishonest about (card)
> **After any card:** Bad news, lies

Knight of Swords

Knight of Swords Reversed

The upright Knight of Swords charges into battle with focus and purpose, but is prepared for inevitable turbulence.

Reversed, this knight may have missed an opportunity, or been far too aggressive in his pursuit of success, leading to bullying behavior, conflict, and cowardly actions.

Questions answered by the reversed Knight of Swords:

Who? A rebellious teen
What? A dispute
Where? A locker room; a "boy's club"
When? Mid-January to Early February; The middle of the school year; The time has come and gone already
Why? "No one heals himself by wounding another." ~St. Ambrose
Yes or No? No

The reversed Knight of Swords as:

...an action?
- Think before you speak
- Back away

...a place in your house?
- A basement bedroom
- A phone charging cable

...a place in your city?
- A schoolyard
- A gym locker room

...a place in the world?
- Portugal
- Austria
- The West coast of South America

...something to eat?
- Food you bought with other people's money
- Meat and eggs

...something to clean?
- Fix holes in the wall

...where to find a missing item?
- Where you last looked - you missed it

...a color? Black, green

...a movie theme? Bullying, aggression
- The Grinch
- Napoleon Dynamite
- The Prom

...a new career?
- Engineering manager
- A job at a high school
- Boss

The reversed Knight of Swords
    Before any card: Thoughtless disregard about (card)
    After any card: Rudeness, aggression

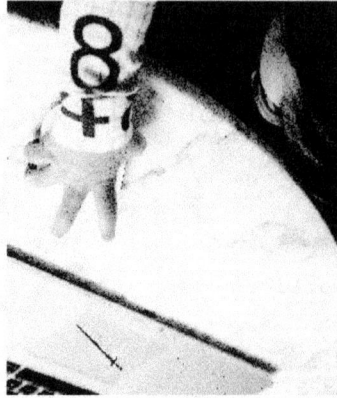

Queen of Swords

Queen of Swords Reversed

The Queen of Swords is self-aware, fiercely individual, and unique. This perfectionism may be a cause of pain or sorrow, however.

Reversed, we see the pain and sorrow come out as an overly pessimistic or critical person. The queen is manipulative, rude, and lacks empathy. Sometimes she is infertile or very confused.

Questions answered by the reversed Queen of Swords:

Who? A malicious woman
What? Miscommunication
Where? A trauma center
When? Mid-September to early October; When you are suffering emotionally
Why? "Just because something isn't a lie does not mean that it isn't deceptive. A liar knows that he is a liar, but one who speaks mere portions of truth in order to deceive is a craftsman of destruction." ~Criss Jami
Yes or No? Probably not

The reversed Queen of Swords as:

...an action?
- Be cautious when sharing information
- Stop lying to yourself about your situation
- Hold back criticism

...a place in your house?
- A window
- The attic

...a place in your city?
- A dorm or sorority
- A strip mall

...a place in the world?
- Las Vegas
- Russia
- Greece
- China

...something to eat?
- Ice
- Liquor

...something to clean?
- The windows
- A box from the attic or high storage

...where to find the missing item?
- At the bottom of a drawer

...a color? black, beige

...a movie theme? Manipulation; criticism
- Trainwreck
- Captain Fantastic

A new career?
- Marketing
- Software Engineer
- Program Manager
- Locksmith

Queen of Swords reversed
> **Before any card:** Someone is being lied to about (card)
> **After any card:** Manipulation; criticism; pessimism

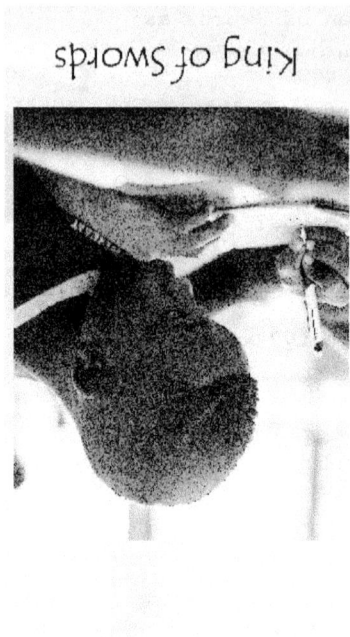
King of Swords

King of Swords reversed

Upright, the King of Swords is kind and helpful, but can be dominating and assertive. However, the king knows what they are talking about.

Reversed, this King is irrational, cynical, and manipulative. It is best to avoid this person, or change your ways if this is yourself.

Questions answered by the reversed King of Swords:

Who? An abusive man
What? A lawsuit
Where? A tyrannical place; a difficult workplace
When? Mid May to early June; After a loss; When the tides turn
Why? "When one with honeyed words but evil mind Persuades the mob, great woes befall the state." ~Euripides
Yes or No? Yes, but be very cautious

The reversed King of Swords as:

...an action?
- Check your facts
- Don't believe everything you hear
- Contact a professional
- Do not take action at this time

...a place in your house?
- The phone
- A high storage area or shelf

...a place in your city?
- The capitol building
- A power plant

...a place in the world?
- Cuba
- Vietnam
- Saudi Arabia
- The UK

...something to eat?
- Steak and potatoes
- Shark fin soup
- Pomegranates
- KFC

...something to clean?
- High shelves
- The entire office and do not ask again until you are done

...where to find the missing item?
- Where you last yelled at someone

...a color? Yellow, brown

...a movie theme? Controlling leader, cold-heartedness
- 1984
- Black Mirror (TV)
- Enemy of the State

...a new career?
- CEO
- Lawyer
- Clergy
- Journalist

King of Swords reversed
> **Before any card:** Be cautious when working with (card)
> **After any card:** Lack of structure; ruthlessness

Pentacles *Reversed*

Pentacles represent earth, money, and the physical and material world that we can see and touch.

When reversed, these cards are typically the darker side of material things, such as greed, infertility, or litter.

Ace of Pentacles

Ace of Pentacles Reversed

Upright, the Ace of Pentacles in a reading is an extremely positive message about an upcoming productive or rewarding period in your life.

Reversed, there is greed, unhealthy decisions, or a period where the financial flow is lacking. You may be so focused on acquiring more *stuff* that you are failing to find gratitude for what you already have.

Questions answered by the reversed Ace of Pentacles:

Who? A greedy person
What? A lost opportunity
Where? In a bank
When? Spring (Northern Hemisphere) or Autumn (Southern Hemisphere); Yesterday
Why? "Earth provides enough to satisfy every man's needs, but not every man's greed." ~Mahatma Gandhi
Yes or No? Maybe

The reversed Ace of Pentacles as:

...an action?
- Take a bath
- Eat yummy food

...a place in your house?
- The garden
- A safe
- A young child's room

...a place in your city?
- The bank
- A big box store
- A fancy hotel
- A resort

...a place in the world?
- The UAE
- A tropical resort
- Australia
- North America

...something to eat?
- Carbs
- A milkshake

...something to clean?
- The safe
- The children's toys

...where to find the missing item?
- In a vault or secure location
- Near the fridge

...a color? Yellow

...a movie theme? Greed; missed opportunity
- Wonder Woman 1984
- The Producers
- Ocean's Eleven

...a new career?
- Wall street broker
- Used car salesman
- News anchor
- business startup

Ace of Pentacles reversed
Before any card: A missed opportunity involving (card)
After any card: Greed; instability

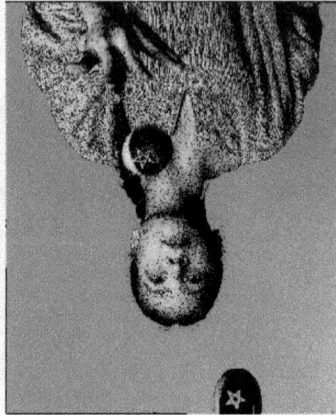

Two of Pentacles Reversed

Upright, the Two of Pentacles is the juggling card. It is about balancing resources, exchanging goods, transferring funds between accounts, or the basic economics of everyday life.

Reversed, there is stress involved in the upright meaning. Perhaps there is a delay in a financial transaction, one's bills are overwhelming, or there is a lack of planning leading to the "balls being dropped."

Questions answered by the reversed Two of Pentacles:

Who? An overwhelmed person; a poor juggler
What? A letter
Where? At a circus; in a ball pit
When? The end of December; two days ago; during times of stress
Why? "To achieve great things, two things are needed: a plan and not quite enough time."
~Leonard Bernstein
Yes or No? Maybe

The reversed Two of Pentacles as:

...an action?
- Focus on one thing at a time
- Double check your finances and plans

...a place in your house?
- The kitchen floor
- Under a desk
- The mailbox

...a place in your city?
- A furniture store
- A sports arena

...a place in the world?
- New York City
- Panama City, FL
- Austin, Texas
- The Ukraine

...something to eat?
- Blueberries
- Brazil nuts

...something to clean?
- Sweep the floors
- Throw out old leftovers

...where to find the missing item?
- On the floor, perhaps rolled under a desk

...a color? Orange, red

...a movie theme? Dropping the balls; financial messes
- Big Fish
- The Greatest Showman
- Dumbo

...a new career?
- Academia
- Warehouse work
- Locksmith
- Author

Two of Pentacles reversed
  Before any card: A lack of balance with (card)
  After any card: poor financial decisions; mistakes

 Three of Pentacles

Three of Pentacles Reversed

The Three of Pentacles upright is about collaboration and mastery, artistic ability, education, and teamwork.

Reversed, this card indicates one hasn't learned from their mistakes, isn't growing or expanding their education, or lacks the commitment necessary to complete a task nor work with a team.

Questions answered by the reversed Three of Pentacles:

Who? An unskilled worker
What? No goals; apathy
Where? Sitting on a bench
When? The beginning of January; when effort is lacking
Why? "Tolerance and apathy are the last virtues of a dying society." ~Aristotle
Yes or No? No

The reversed Three of Pentacles as:

...an action?
- Engage in a networking activity
- Watch how-to videos
- Take the first step toward completing a project

...a place in your house?
- An unfinished project
- The garage
- Unhung artwork

...a place in your city?
- Auto repair shop
- An art studio
- A construction company

...a place in the world?
- Black Hills, SD
- Morocco
- Spain
- Bermuda

...something to eat?
- Rice
- Take-out

...something to clean?
- A workstation or crafts area
- Complete an unfinished project

...where to find the missing item?
- Where you last gave up on a project

...a color? Dark blue, beige

...a movie theme? Mistakes; apathy; no goals
- Lost in Translation
- Everything Must Go
- La La Land

...a new career?
- Outpost work
- Park ranger
- Accountant
- Production line work
- Tree trimmer

Three of Pentacles reversed
Before any card: An unwillingness to learn (card)
After any card: Apathy; a lack of goals

Four of Pentacles

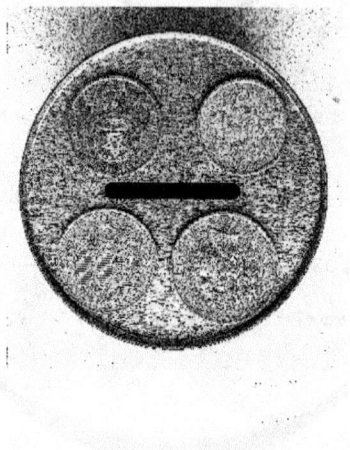

Four of Pentacles Reversed

Upright, the Four of Pentacles is the money lover, one who clutches at material goods and does not let go. Although this card represents a pleasant chapter of your life where your needs are met, it is also a warning not to be selfish about what you have acquired.

Reversed, it is the exacerbation of the upright meanings. One might be so comfortable that they are reckless with their resources, or they may be extra greedy, hoarding money they don't need to hoard.

Questions answered by the reversed Four of Pentacles:

Who? The big spender
What? An extravagant purchase
Where? At a shopping center
When? The middle of January; When you make a donation
Why? "Hoard food and it rots. Hoard money and you rot. Hoard power and the nation rots." ~Chuck Palahniuk
Yes or No? No

The reversed Four of Pentacles as:

...an action?
- Make a donation to a charity
- Buy yourself something nice

...a place in your house?
- A trophy shelf
- The safe
- The pantry
- A storage unit

...a place in your city?
- The shopping mall
- A brokerage

...a place in the world?
- China
- Las Vegas, NV
- Edmonton, Alberta
- London, England

...something to eat?
- An expensive organic restaurant
- Eggo waffles

...something to clean?
- Empty out a bank account

...where to find the missing item?
- Someone else has it

...a color? purple; gold; green

...a movie theme? Hoarding; spending too much
- Brewster's Millions
- The Big Short
- Parasite

...a new career?
- Grant writer
- Business reporter
- Foundation or nonprofit work
- Financial executive

Four of Pentacles reversed
Before any card: The financial control of (card)
After any card: giving away resources; hoarding

Five of Pentacles

Five of Pentacles Reversed

The Five of Pentacles upright is about looking
for opportunities when you are feeling unstable. It is
also about changing from a mindset of scarcity to
gratitude.

Reversed, the opportunity is found, and there
might be a slight improvement in finances, the end of a
difficult situation, or a financial or physical
recovery.

Questions answered by the reversed Five of Pentacles:

Who? Someone in recovery
What? Employment; security
Where? Inside
When? The end of April; When things start looing
up
Why? "Always hold on to the material things with
open hands" ~G Swiss
Yes or No? Maybe

The reversed Five of Pentacles as:

...an action?
- Be careful with newfound money
- Show gratitude to someone

...a place in your house?
- The window
- The medicine cabinet

...a place in your city?
- A rehab center
- A hospital
- An ATM

...a place in the world?
- Malibu, CA
- New Zealand
- Iceland
- Japan

...something to eat?
- Leafy green salad
- Eggs
- Seafood

...something to clean?
- Make the bed
- The medicine cabinet

...where to find the missing item?
- In the bathroom cabinet
- Up high

...a color? blue

...a movie theme? Recovery, finding hope
- Silver Linings Playbook
- 50/50
- Inside Out

A new career?
- Substance abuse counselor
- Physical trainer
- Bus driver
- Bookkeeper

Five of Pentacles reversed
>**Before any card:** Overcoming a difficult period of (card)
>**After any card:** recovery; financial breakthrough

Six of Pentacles

Six of Pentacles Reversed

The upright Six of Pentacles brings us to a position where we either have enough resources to give back, or we are finally open to receiving gifts. Whether you are the giver or the receiver will depend on where you are in your life, but in either situation the six is about generosity and favors.

Reversed, there is a lack of generosity happening, or an abuse of power. If gifts are given, there may be strings attached. Someone isn't helping someone else when they can or should.

Questions answered by the reversed Six of Pentacles:

Who? A miser
What? No financial support
Where? In a selfish person's possession
When? The Beginning of May; When help is requested
Why? "Selfishness is not living as one wishes to live, it is asking others to live as one wishes to live." ~Oscar Wilde
Yes or No? Yes

The reversed Six of Pentacles as:

...an action?
- Give more
- Ask someone for help

...a place in your house?
- The safe
- The bedroom closet

...a place in your city?
- A church
- A casino resort
- A country club

...a place in the world?
- Connecticut
- Uganda
- Portugal
- Vatican City

...something to eat?
- Soup or pudding
- Sloppy Joes

...something to clean?
- The master bedroom and closet
- The office

...where to find the missing item?
- In your personal belongings; on your person

...a color? Green, orange

...a movie theme? Selfishness, inequality
- Period. End of Sentence
- Slumdog Millionaire
- Lion

A new career?
- Software Developer
- Stock or mortgage broker
- Secretary

Six of Pentacles reversed
Before any card: There will be no assistance with (card)
After any card: Selfishness; inequality

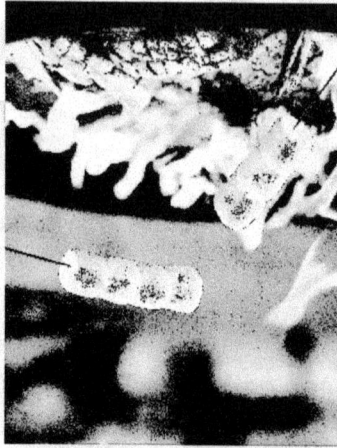

Seven of Pentacles

Seven of Pentacles Reversed

The Seven of Pentacles upright is about patience assessment, perseverance and hard work.

Reversed, it's almost always negative. You can look at the reversed seven as the opposite of hard work. It could be bad business management, an inability to complete what you've started, or not getting any benefits from your labor.

Questions answered by the reversed Seven of Pentacles:

Who? One who is unable to retire
What? A failed investment; a debt
Where? At a failing business
When? The middle of May; Seven months ago; when the investment loses money
Why? "We often miss opportunity because it's dressed in overalls and looks like work" ~Thomas A. Edison
Yes or No? No

The reversed Seven of Pentacles as:

...an action?
- Change your mind
- Do not take action now

...a place in your house?
- Dirt
- Unused pots and pans
- A pile of unpaid bills

...a place in your city?
- An empty construction site
- An abandoned building

...a place in the world?
- California
- India
- Barcelona, Spain
- The Suez canal
- Edinburgh, Scotland

...something to eat?
- Hot dogs
- Pie

...something to clean?
- The space around you right now

...where to find the missing item?
- Where you were last sitting or lying down

...a color? Light blue

...a movie theme? Laziness; bad business management
- 101 Dalmations
- Office Space
- Startup.com

...a new career?
- Line stand-in
- Tester - food, hotel, video game, etc

Seven of Pentacles reversed
> **Before any card:** Bad business decisions about (card)
> **After any card:** Failed investments; laziness

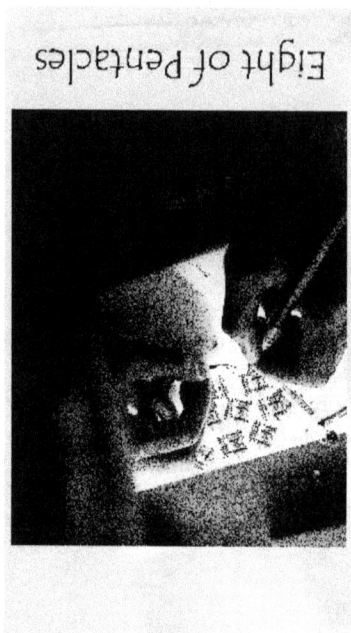

Eight of Pentacles

Eight of Pentacles Reversed

The upright Eight of Pentacles is a skilled craftsperson or apprentice. This card is about patience, hard work, and pride over one's studies and work accomplishments.

Reversed, it is the negatives of school and work. It could be a boring job, mediocre work efforts, a lack of interest in studies or business, or underemployment.

Questions answered by the reversed Eight of Pentacles:

Who? Someone in a dead end career
What? Poor quality work
Where? At the workplace
When? The end of August; When you get a boring project; 8 months
Why? "Dead-end roads don't mean you've come to your end, just means you need to take a different detour." ~Anthony Liccione
Yes or No? No

The reversed Eight of Pentacles as:

...an action?
- Find a new fulfilling career
- Take a break from a project
- Watch out for shabby work

...a place in your house?
- A cluttered desk or room
- A collection of school supplies

...a place in your city?
- The pub during the daytime
- A cat café
- The movie theatre

...a place in the world?
- South Africa
- The Czech Republic
- Spain
- Slovakia

...something to eat?
- Chicken legs
- Canned food
- Fried cauliflower
- Stew

...something to clean?
- A pile of clutter
- Your desk

...where to find the missing item?
- In a junk drawer

...a color? blue, purple

...a movie theme? Boredom; underemployment
- The Breakfast Club
- The Grand Budapest Hotel
- Tiny Furniture

...a new career?
- Technical Support representative
- Office assistant
- Dog groomer
- Student

Eight of Pentacles reversed
> **Before any card:** There is a lack of success in (card)
> **After any card:** Boredom; underemployment

Nine of Pentacles

Nine of Pentacles reversed

Upright, the Nine denotes abundance, wisdom, luxury, and the obtainment of material goods. The person depicted in this nine has gained independent financial success and is now at a place where they should be seeking companionship to share it with.

Reversed, this person is dependent upon others for their financial survival. They may be marrying for money, living off their parents, or they are overworked and underpaid.

Questions answered by the reversed Nine of Pentacles:

Who? A dependent; a gold-digger
What? The lack of elegance; superficiality
Where? At someone else's house
When? The beginning of September; During a financial setback
Why? "Dependency breeds contempt." ~Marty Rubin
Yes or No? No

The reversed Nine of Pentacles as:

...an action?
- Change your plans
- Be realistic
- Get a job
- Support yourself

...a place in your house?
- Another person's possessions
- A pet's ashes
- A makeup case
- Unused exercise equipment

...a place in your city?
- A clearance store
- Downtown
- An abandoned lodge

...a place in the world?
- The Maldives
- Aruba
- Amsterdam
- Las Vegas, NV

...something to eat?
- Poultry
- Celery
- Food someone gave you

...something to clean?
- Someone else's stuff

...where to find the missing item?
- In the chicken coop
- With someone else's belongings

...a color? Red

...a movie theme? Dependency, reproductive issues
- Baby Mama
- Pretty Woman
- The Wedding Singer

...a new career?
- Marry for money
- Hobo
- Financial advisor
- Duck hunter
- Surrogate

Nine of Pentacles reversed
    Before any card: A toxic dependency on (card)
    After any card: deceit; superficiality; infertility

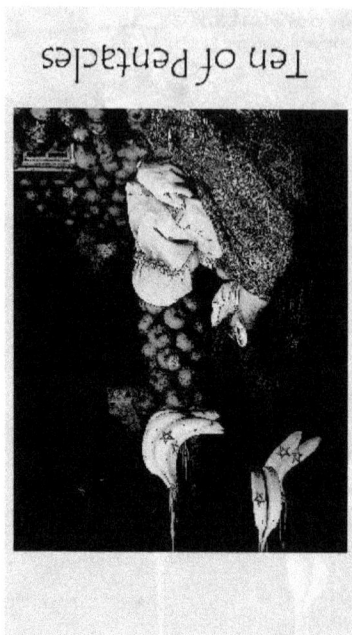

Ten of Pentacles

Ten of Pentacles Reversed

The Ten of Pentacles upright is about fortune, legacy, and inheritance. This card depicts the epitome of wealth, the highest level of career success, or a completed family tree.

Reversed, it is generally the worst-case scenario for finances, such as a disaster, bankruptcy, issues with inheritances or wills, divorce, or money loss.

Questions answered by the reversed Ten of Pentacles:

> **Who?** Someone going through a divorce or bankruptcy
> **What?** A disputed financial transaction
> **Where?** Behind the bank
> **When?** The middle of September; During a reading of a will; At the end of a life stage
> **Why?** "It's easy to meet expenses – everywhere we go, there they are." ~Anonymous
> **Yes or No?** No

The reversed Ten of Pentacles as:

...an action?
- Deal with difficult family
- Dispute a transaction
- Take care of your business affairs

...a place in your house?
- Where you've stored the will
- Symbols of your culture or heritage

...a place in your city?
- A hospice center
- A divorce lawyer
- A planned neighborhood

...a place in the world?
- Los Angeles, CA
- Shanghai, China
- London, England
- Russia

...something to eat?
- Fried eggs
- Noodles
- Frozen food
- fruitcake

...something to clean?
- Clean out your social media friends list
- Items from your culture

...where to find the missing item?
- Someone older than you has it

...a color? blue, green

...a movie theme? Debt; financial disaster; family trouble
- American Hustle
- Get shorty
- We're the Millers

...a new career?
- Doctor
- Laborer
- Uber driver
- Estate planner

Ten of Pentacles reversed
> **Before any card:** Refrain from financial dealings with (card)
> **After any card:** Debt; bankruptcy; will disputes

Page of Pentacles

Page of Pentacles Reversed

Upright, the Page of Pentacles is a young, studious individual. This is a card about going back to school or engaging in activism for a sustainable future.

Reversed, this page is unfocused, disorganized, immature, and unrealistic. The reversed page might be the bearer of bad news, or a warning that you are living a champagne life on a lemonade budget.

Questions answered by the reversed Page of Pentacles:

Who? A careless young person
What? A lack of money
Where? An amusement park
When? Spring (Northern Hemisphere) or Fall (Southern Hemisphere); When the money runs out; after college
Why? "Never spend your money before you have earned it." ~Thomas Jefferson
Yes or No? No

The reversed Page of Pentacles as:

...an action?
- Follow through on your commitments
- Make a budget

...a place in your house?
- The kitchen counter

...a place in your city?
- A juvenile detention center
- A university financial services department

...a place in the world?
- Rhode Island
- Reno, NV
- Madison, WI
- the South pacific

...something to eat?
- Pizza
- Unnatural foods

...something to clean?
- Check your credit score
- Delete old email contacts

...where to find the missing item?
- Where you last partied too hard

...a color? Purple, red, green

...a movie theme? Bad news; immaturity
- The Hangover
- Idiocracy
- Step Brothers

...a new career?
- Bike repair
- Something in the cannabis industry
- Nurse or Legal assistant

Page of Pentacles reversed
> **Before any card:** A lack of common sense about (card)
> **After any card:** Bad news; being unfocused

Knight of Pentacles Reversed

Upright, the Knight of Pentacles is a guard or another type of stationary protector. While ambitious, this knight surveys the land and chooses the best courses of action to take before making a move, making this card is about practicality and dependability.

Reversed, the knight is impatient, irresponsible, or doesn't finish what he or she starts. This card could also indicate a problem with earning money, or someone who is greedy and materialistic.

Questions answered by the reversed Knight of Pentacles:

Who? An unreliable person
What? Apathy
Where? A large shopping center
When? Mid-April to early May; When you've given up
Why? "Many sophisticated, intelligent people lack wisdom and common sense." ~Joyce Meyer
Yes or No? Not now

The reversed Knight of Pentacles as:

...an action?
- Rest
- Let it go
- Resist laziness
- Stop obsessing

...a place in your house?
- The pet(s) area
- The living room

...a place in your city?
- An ice cream shop
- The horse races
- A cemetery

...a place in the world?
- Melbourne
- Louisville, KY
- Thailand
- The South Pacific

...something to eat?
- Bread
- Wine
- Snacks bought from a retail counter

...something to clean?
- The fish pond
- The living room floor

...where to find the missing item?
- Out back

...a color? Blue; green; purple

...a movie theme? Complacency; unreliable narrators
- Memento
- The Wrong Missy
- The Girl on the Train

A new career?
- Retail
- Cable installer
- Politician

Knight of Pentacles reversed
> **Before any card:** Promises are not being kept about (card)
> **After any card:** Disloyalty; lack of common sense

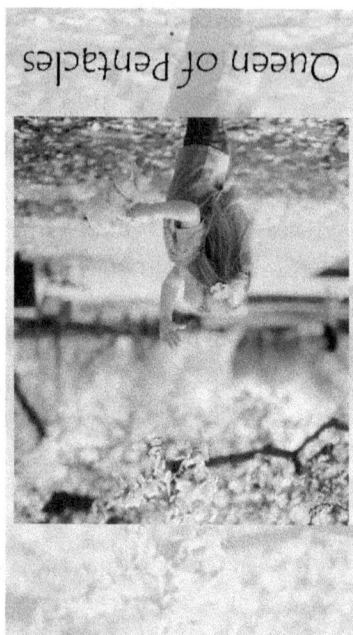

Queen of Pentacles

Queen of Pentacles Reversed

Upright, the Queen of Pentacles is a nurturing parent who is down-to-Earth, approachable, practical, and successful in business and at home.

Reversed, the queen is self-centered, smothering, possessive, manipulative, or is an otherwise bad mother.

Questions answered by the reversed Queen of Pentacles:

Who? A cruel woman
What? Troubles in business or relationships
Where? Your physical environment
When? Mid December to early January; When a manipulator arrives
Why? "What you feed will flourish. What you neglect will die." ~Unknown
Yes or No? No

The Reversed Queen of Pentacles as:

...an action?
- Watch for difficult relationships
- Spend time in nature
- Seek help

...a place in your house?
- Mother's room

...a place in your city?
- The ER
- The Boss or Principal's office
- A creditor
- A wealthy neighborhood

...a place in the world?
- China
- Russia
- Poland
- Laos

...something to eat?
- Popsicle
- Egg in the hole
- Leftover cake

...something to clean?
- Mother's space or room
- A giant mess

...where to find the missing item?
- Buried under important items

...a color? Orange, black

...a movie theme? Smothering, a difficult woman
- The Meddler
- The Guilt Trip
- Florence Foster Jenkins

...a new career?
- Web developer
- Realtor
- Preschool teacher
- Grandmother

Queen of Pentacles reversed
   Before any card: A gross misunderstanding about (card)
   After any card: A difficult woman; a manipulator

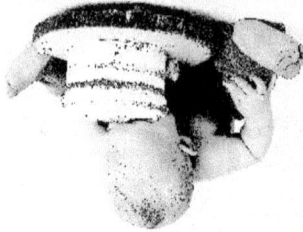

King of Pentacles

King of Pentacles

Upright, the King of Pentacles is powerful and successful, but also conservative and miserly. The king is a great dad, and generous when there is a reward in return.

Reversed, this King might be unsuccessful in business, corrupt, broke, possibly a gambler, and a terrible father.

Questions answered by the reversed King of Pentacles:

Who? A greedy, materialistic person
What? A corrupt business
Where? A casino or house of ill repute
When? Mid-August to early September; When the business is in the red
Why? "An unsuccessful person feels obliged to praise himself all the time because in order to feel happy, he must compensate for his failure in a virtual way!" ~Mehmet Murat ildan
Yes or No? Maybe

The reversed King of Pentacles as:

...an action?
- Ask yourself whether what you're doing pleases your soul or your wallet

...a place in your house?
- The garbage can

...a place in your city?
- A closed up retail shop or restaurant
- A failing business
- A vacant lot

...a place in the world?
- Morocco
- Cyprus
- Greece
- Israel

...something to eat?
- Messy junk food, such as cheese puffs or nachos
- Take-out

...something to clean?
- The office
- The TV room

...where to find the missing item?
- Near trash

...a color? Red, blue, orange

...a movie theme? failure; business corruption
- The Wolf of Wall Street
- Ready Player One
- Planet of the Apes

...a new career?
- Pharmaceutical industry
- College admissions; college leadership
- Management
- Parent

King of Pentacles reversed
> **Before any card:** Be wary of extortion or failure in (card)
> **After any card:** Corruption; haste; greed

Acknowledgements

Thanks to everyone who bought or browsed my first book, *Applied Tarot*. It's overwhelming to publish the first tome in a series, but the encouragement from that little book enabled me to write its sister, *Applied Runes*, this sequel, and the next planned Applied Divination book, *Applied Tasseography*.

This book is dedicated to my husband Oscar, my kids Margaret, David, and Jack, and my new puppy Sherlock, whose difficult personality delayed this book's release by several months, but was an adorable distraction.

Image Credits

Images edited with permission by Emily Paper.

The Fool - Sergey Gimburg & Alexander Dummer
The Magician - Gabe Pierce
The High Priestess - Purnachandra Rao Podilapu
The Empress - Omid Armin
The Emperor - Valeria Zoncoll
The Hierophant - Walter Gadea-Zesab
The Lovers - Travis Grossen
The Chariot - Blake Meyer
Strength - Mohamed Nohassi
The Hermit - Charles Deluvi
Wheel of Fortune - Emma Roordarl
Justice - Bady Abbas
The Hanged Man - Annie Spratt
Death - Marcos Paulo-Prado
Temperance - Kelli McClintock
The Devil - Jomjakkapat Parrueng
The Tower - Ryan Fields
The Star - Lubomirkin
The Moon - Daiga Ellaby
The Sun - Gabby Orcutt & marko Blazevi
Judgement - Kate Indra
The World - Christian Bowen & Danielle Gehler

Swords
Page   - Andriyko Podil
Knight - Fas Khan
Queen - Charles Deluvio
King   - Santi Vedri & Tingey Injury Law Firm
Ace   - Ria Alfana
Two   - Oliver Twist & Mutzii
Three - Wendy Scofield
Four   - Daniele Levis-Pelusi
Five   - Dominik Scyth

Six - Steve Douglas
Seven - Nick Karvounis
Eight - Mak
Nine - Bernard 3
Ten - Greg Evans

Wands
Page - Alexander Dummer
Knight - Janko Ferlic
Queen - Jai Hill
King - Ariel
Ace - Carlo Linares

Two - Dana Cristea
Three - Filip Mroz
Four - Murilo Viviani
Five - Annie Spratt
Six - Wan San Yip
Seven - Ayodeji Alabi
Eight - Kaung Myat-Min
Nine - Luiza Braun
Ten - Annie Spratt

Pentacles
Page - Gift Habeshaw
Knight - Arseny Togulev
Queen - Karl Frederckson
King - Henley Design Studio
Ace - Camila Waz
Two - Alexey Turenko
Three - Robert Collins
Four - Mitchell Luo
Five - Casey Horner & Muhammad Muzamil
Six - Andriyko Podil
Seven - Christian Bowen
Eight - This is Engineering Raeng Q
Nine - Senjuti Kundu
Ten - Arif Riyanto

Cups
Page - Clarene Lalata & Clarissa Carbun
Knight - Annie Spratt
Queen - Yehor milohrods
King - Luke Michael & Paul Hanaoka
Ace - Jelleke Vanooteghem
Two - Nathan Dumlao
Three - Pablo Merchan-Montes
Four - Artem Beliaikin
Five - Nomao Saeki
Six - Chris Jarvis
Seven - Eric Prouzet & Mariana Dal Chic
Eight - Nrd
Nine - Sidney Pearce
Ten - Jonathan Borba

About the Author

After the pandemic proved that the tech industry was not built for women, Emily Paper retired from the industry and returned to her love of claircognizance and the occult. Today, she is a divination and Feng Shui specialist working on a master's degree in Smashing the Patriarchy, or something along those lines.

With over 35 years of random fortune telling experience, it took losing a set of car keys to inspire her to write the first book in this series, *Applied Tarot*.

Emily lives in Washington State with her husband, two cats, and new puppy Sherlock. Any money they earn either goes to the dog or to the college bursar's office for their three college-aged children.

She can be found wandering around social media, and at www.emilypaper.com

This doggo stole my time, my routine, and all my money. Awwww, but I forgive the little silly billy!

Applied Tasseography

An Excessively Practical Guide to Interpreting Tea Leaves

What movie should you watch when a dog shows up at the bottom of your cup?

You should watch the **Truman Show!**

I will never not recommend The Truman Show.

Follow emilypaper.com for more information!

www.ingramcontent.com/pod-product-compliance
Lightning Source LLC
Chambersburg PA
CBHW060843280326
41934CB00007B/899